Scratching Against the Fabric

poems from the
Bridgewater International Poetry Festival 2013

Stan Galloway, editor
Timothy Wisniewski, associate editor

Englewood, NJ

ISBN 978-1-936373-50-5

© 2015 Stan Galloway. All rights reserved. No part of this publication may be reproduced or transmitted in any form or by any means, electronic or mechanical, without permission in writing from the publisher. Requests for permission to make copies of any part of this work should be e-mailed to info@unboundcontent.com.

Published in the United States by Unbound Content, LLC, Englewood, NJ.

Cover art: © 2015 KC Bosch

The poems in this collection are all original and previously unpublished with the exception of those listed in the credits page at the end of the volume.

SCRATCHING AGAINST THE FABRIC
First edition 2015

Contents

Introduction 11
Tongue 15
Notes from a Rhenish Mission: 3 17
Cape Doctor 18
Senjaray, Afghanistan 21
Rainbow Bridge 22
Eating Contest in a Third World Diner 23
Paris-Shiraz 24
Stolen Rivers 26
Coming Home 27
To Do: 28
Who Knew [how to describe] 29
The Gargantuan Muffin Beauty Contest 30
Leaving Elkton 32
enter the house: desert ode 33
Letter to My Grandfather 38
Wandering Jew 39
Continental Drift 40
Fable with Pekin Ducks 43
Out Here in the Country 44
Carolina Handler 46
Alabama Sunshine 48
New World Finches 49
Limbo 50
Collapse of the Silver Bridge 54
The Meaning of Melanin 55
Hopscotch Pedigree 58

Hudson County Girl	59
Millennium Retribution in Key West	60
Somewhere in New Mexico	62
Big-Rig Through Stolen Night	63
The Wolf at the Door	64
Guided by Stars and Glass	66
Set Adrift	68
Failed Romance	69
Been Loving All My Life	70
for Imad	72
Good Morning	74
Wishing Tree, 6 June 1977	75
The Last Night	76
Carnival	77
Overheard at a Bar in NYC	78
The Harbor Inn	80
Night Vigil	82
Woman at the Auction House	83
Capote and Brando Talk Over Drinks	84
World's First Blues	86
Listening Ears	87
No Country for Young "I"	88
Invasion of the Body Snatchers	89
Teary Queene	90
Stranger	92
My Rappaccini's Daughter	93
Before and After	94
Rose M. Singer	96
Shane	98

Earth-Two Sonnet	99
walt whitman: a tribute	100
Baudelaire	103
Valleys Breathe, Heaven & Earth	104
Move Together	104
Dead Poet in the Passenger Seat	105
Pilgrimage	107
Scholarship Girl, 1953	108
A Room of One's Own	109
Fire Builder	111
The (Poe)t	113
Poetic Vision	114
Julian, in Her Cell: 1405	115
The Cellar Door	117
Disappearance, 26 July 1977	118
The Changeling	119
After Sandy Hook	121
Notes from a Rhenish Mission: 20	122
Mannlicher Rackenakt	123
Starship Tahiti	125
how?	126
Waist-deep in Sand	127
Swim	129
Battery	134
Anthem	138
Buffeted	140
Metallica Burns on the Altar of the Viking Rockstar	142
Well-Regulated Dumplings	144
Are Going Upwards	144

Domestic Garden 145
Notes from a Rhenish Mission: 18 146
I've Heard of You 147
One True Story 148
Splinter 150
For K 151
heart beat 153
Revisiting Past's Seasons 156
God's Watermark 157
Oceans of Love 159
My Father's Frying Pan 160
Mama 161
Grandmother Magic, 13 August 1977 162
The One Breath 163
Acknowledgments 165

Introduction

This book comes from a small beginning, a small idea with a big reach. The Bridgewater International Poetry Festival began on a cold January day, in a little town in the Shenandoah Valley. This is where I teach. Increasingly, Bridgewater College intends to create global citizens, and part of my job is to find ways to make that happen. I like that challenge. While many students travel abroad as part of their education, many others cannot bear that cost. So, I am convinced that we must bring the world to Bridgewater.

After a year of e-mail (no budget, therefore no print advertising), thirty-eight poets from a variety of backgrounds gathered for four days to read, hear, and discuss their own poetry. Some of those poets traveled internationally for the event; some, who tried to attend but could not for a number of reasons, participated via an internet connection or through a recording sent ahead of time. Representatives from four continents and from six decades gave a rich heritage across ages and landscapes.

The idea behind this book was to create a source of revenue for international poets who could not attend for financial reasons. The poets in this book have agreed to allow all profits from the sale of this book to create a scholarship fund to assist poets in attending future festivals. The plan is for this event to be repeated every two years.

The poems here were all presented at the festival in 2013. They represent excellent expressions of personalities and ideas in an ever-tighter world. Czeslaw Milosz has said that "on a planet growing ever smaller, increasingly we dine on the same cultural dishes" (Foreword. *Miracle Fair: Selected Poems of Wislawa Szymborska*. Tr. Joanna Trzeciak. New York: Norton, 2002. 2). *Scratching Against the Fabric* samples a number of cultures, by no means comprehensively nor in a balanced way, but it is a start, a dish, if you will, on the global table of poets.

In the opening poem, "Tongue," we are reminded of the global nature of art. Phillippa Yaa de Villiers appended a note to me with the poem pointing out, "English could just as well be substituted for French, Portuguese or Spanish." For this anthology, we are constrained to employ English because of our own limited exposure to other languages. That is to our own detriment. While some non-English words and phrases might be employed in poems written in English, a reader should have no trouble understanding them in context. While some poets, like T.S. Eliot, are phenomenal linguists, many readers are not. For this reason, we employ English as our medium of expression. But even our English is not the same around the globe, and so I've allowed matters of dispute—such as *color* or *colour*, or the American preference for the comma inside quotation marks and the British preference for outside—to fall to the poet's choice.

The title of this anthology is taken from Lesley Wheeler's "Scholarship Girl, 1953." The phrase evokes the desire to push against those forces at work to bring unwanted conformity, sometimes very soft controls, as in language (Don Maclennan's "Notes from a Rhenish Mission: 18") or more obvious assertions in identity (Jacqueline Bishop's "Fire Builder") and against social conditions (J Indigo Eriksen's "enter the house: desert ode"); or all three when Kate Lahey says in "The Meaning of Melanin," "Words like *black* and *white* / Are made-up pests."

The poems in *Scratching Against the Fabric* talk of the world, of love, of freedom, but also of constraint, and of disappointment. These are global emotions and responses. These poems range from intellectual to therapeutic, from a few lines to a few pages, from contentment to concern. Many of these poets have published books, and I encourage you, the reader, to follow and acquire the work of the ones who impress you.

Bon appétit.
Stan Galloway, editor

Tongue
Phillippa Yaa de Villiers

The lord said in my house there are many
mansions and it's true. My neighbour lives in
Afrikaans and the one on the other
side is in Shangaan and I live in the
house of this poem. When we meet, me and my
neighbours we meet in English, which we
all wear with our own styles. English is the market
and also the law like the time when
Sister Mavis's druggie son stole from
me and was caught; we heard the story
and the apology, there in front
of the magistrate, all dressed in our best
English.

English forced us out of our own house of
Language. Burnt down the village, bombed the city.
Missionaries came after to dress our
naked memories, to recraft a path
to God. The language that we own is the
English that they loaned, reworked to fit our mouths
our traditional attire and our fine tailored trousers:
smart and also hand me down.

For Corinna handing out hot dogs at
the Sunday school barbecue, her gold tooth
glinting as she gives and gives, English is
a too tight dress that shows off too much and
Teacher Suzanne's English is too big and
drags along the floor; Andile's English
is outside   beating at the door.
For friends from India to Aotearoa, from Kenya to St Kitts
English sits in our mouth like a new set of teeth—
not like the ones the dentist makes—
our English really fits because we are native English speakers
and our English has been curried and spiced and tossed

Scratching Against the Fabric

into a nice salad with pineapple.
We were torn apart from each other and we want to go back home,
not back to where we were born-born
but back to a time when we were born in a tongue,
a tongue we can now use to become one: to find our tribe,
and become one.

Notes from a Rhenish Mission: 3
Don Maclennan

The Rhenish Mission, 1860:
dwellings, store, church, school.
One building has survived:
on its stoep they're chopping down
a peppercorn that split the paving stones
and cracked the whitewashed wall.
Its last use was for sheep, fleas leaping
in black clouds from the ankle-deep dung.

They prise off the old mud plaster
which still smells of grass, and sounds
like foreign vowels and consonants as it breaks—
'Nun danket alle Gott'—
And falls around their feet.

Cape Doctor
Toni Stuart

wind
tell me your stories

tell me thoughts you
thrust across night's soot sky
tell me truth you
traipse through dreams to find
as you sweep
through windows
and send curtains billowing
into veils

wind
tell me your stories

of cries—without faces—
ringing out in the unforgiving
silence of a city
seething at its seams

seeping with anger
of palms too scared to
touch their
pain
afraid they will crumble
never to be built again

and tell me your stories

tell me tears you
you never cry,
tell me fears you
store in silent pockets of
hands that wipe out whole
cities with one word.
as autumn paints a city
amber, you strip the green from

her skin throw it to
spring; tango with trees
and thrust leaves across a wanting sky
you burrow and funnel

through our sleeping
morph into song of ocean
heave against our walls

tell me of the love you
stir in an instant to render us
skinless
and tell me their stories

a man with cinnamon
hands who broke soil to grow
sun on a long stem;
who singed cotton nappies drying
them across his
oven to show his love for my tears;
pushed back disease and
death so he could witness
my life
grandfather, whose stories i never got to hear

a woman whose
thoughts were too fast for her
tongue
who taught her son love is
gentle orange firm
who they didn't name me after
but whose heart i inherited
still
grandmother, i remember your face
but not the sound of your voice
or the words that stitched you together
wind

Scratching Against the Fabric

where have you carried them
        buried them?
do their songs sleep
easy in your folds. could you sing
them to me?

you race against yourself,
from False Bay to Atlantic Coast
return in time for breakfast
to cocoon me in your breath
as you ease me from sleep
but questions
quell this heart's peace

wind, tell me your stories
so I may know
the other half of
me

Author's Note: Cape Doctor *is the local term given to Cape Town's South-Easter wind. The wind's ability to clear out the smog and pollution in the city's sky, resulted in the name.*

Senjaray, Afghanistan
Sara Robinson

The book, found, dusty and torn
still had its pages intact.
Leftover from the old library,
it would start the new one.
Pages as seeds to start a new oasis.

A school closed for years had a chance to open for the winter.
The fighting groups battled tough
through a hot summer—the violent season.
Grenades that had found young bodies and
abandoned houses were silent.
The school's role as fortress was finished—
Walls now only holding secrets and bullet remains.

Daily threats of mortars and small arms attacks
kept parents and neighbors panicked.
Children, dimmed and desperate, fought everyone as the   enemy.
They used guns too big to handle,
too heavy to aim, but it didn't matter.
Their chests absorbed the blasts and the kicks
killed by those that knowledge threatens.

They have barely the winter to get the school back in order.
Teachers will come, the leader said. I have money and
can pay them to live right here.
Our own will teach our own.
Our village will have smart kids and they can fight
the enemy with stealth and tactics.

Back along a shattered wall, shelves leaning but in place,
a soldier put the found book on its side next to a helmet.
Using his blood-stained scarf, he gave a gentle wipe to the cover.
War and Peace
At last somewhere it might be read.

Rainbow Bridge
WF Lantry

—Beijing *Qingming Scroll*, 12 C

If you could weave straight beams into loose curves
or even as an arch across a stream,
the ax hewn wood spokeshaved by oiled blades
and lifted up in cantilevered weight,
balanced an instant as the joints are pinned
by cloven iron spikes at hammer height,

you'd still require ways to lash them tight,
and no hemp rope would meet your long term need.
You'd have to be inventive. Green bamboo
grows everywhere along the banks. Just hack
the rampant stalks at ground level. Then split
each cane lengthwise with your machete. Tear

the halves apart. Split each again. Prepare
to watch your skin turn raw and start to bleed,
but don't give up until the loose strands seem
as light as cottonwood in summer wind.
Start weaving them as one. A figure eight
will serve as end-whip. Tension it, and wet

the whole length equally. Pinned joints offset
each other. Start beneath them, leaving slack
to bind the next along the line, then fit
successive timbers down. Check level, true,
and square, then let it dry until green fades
and cover all with any paint that serves.

Eating Contest in a Third World Diner
KC Bosch

That was fast; I bet you couldn't eat another.
You pay if I do?
If that's a bet count me in too.

Red poppies and Moorish domes
in the bright midday sun,
like a motion picture
viewed through green glass
and air conditioned cigar smoke.
The big Benz parked next to the empty donkey cart,
fries with gravy, *arroz con pollo*,
cold Coke in 12 oz bottles, wrapped
sugar cubes on a tray.
Spinning bug on the china is actually
a ceiling fan doing its best.
Big steaks devoured by
overfed child travelers.

Paris-Shiraz
Sana Khalesi

beneath the spell of your hazel eyes breathing
when right-or-left choices of
death or dying
arise
a glare
a caution
with a respite on the cushion of your lips
or when
the innocence of your heart
rips
my only belonging
and departs
with a 4-foot hole
in my still stale moth-eaten soul

oh trail me
regale me
seek this sick-me
with your equilateral longing legs
seek your poison snogs
on my lost-in-the-smoke-and-ashes lungs
TRASH me!
and turn this crude cremation
into Louisiana Iris
and TRASH
all the bridges
from Shiraz to Paris
and TRASH
memories, reveries, treacheries
all gracious photos
and post-hardcore songs of EMERY

while nodding your hideous head
while sipping your afternoon coffee,
while listening to your only insanity-plea
peering to your vicious voice, uttering:
"oh oui oui!"

there's no ME,
NO WE!
and you are propelling
another mistress, Dionysus
with curly creamy short-cut hair
smiling
lost in her castle-in-the-air
smiting
peeling avocado pear
with your tender solicitous care

and I—
now dust—
beneath your steps
and missteps
giving an ear to Joan Baez's "Diamonds & Rust":
"… smiling out the window
      of the crummy hotel over Washington Square"
I dare
I dare you
pretermit me
by giving your fictitious look
a more factual gloss
in my loss!

Stolen Rivers
for Chiwoniso Maraire
Phillippa Yaa de Villiers

We Africans came to Berlin to sing
and recite poetry. We had an agenda:
remembering our anthems of loss,
galloping, consuming,
the pillage, the cries
like forest fires, like haunted children,
how can we, how can we even
begin to redress?
Enraged, we wanted revenge
and then, Chiwoniso, you stepped on the stage and
you opened your mouth and
every stolen river of platinum and gold
poured out of your mouth in song;
your voice etched us out of the night
and doubled the light in each of us.
You restored all the treasure-houses
from Benin to Zimbabwe, Mapungubwe to Cairo;
Africa moved its golden bones,
shook off its heavy chains
and danced again.
That night I thought
if only
love could purchase bread,
Africans would not be hungry.

Coming Home
Holley Watts

In September 1967 I came back to the Real World.
From the train station I caught a cab to my parents' home
but along the way I must have been commenting a lot on
how different ... how long ... how cool ... how ...
Lady, where have you been?!
Vietnam, I chirped.

A quick look in his rear view mirror and
I pressed hard into the back of the seat
where he couldn't reach me to throw me out.
he veered his cab toward the curb.

The cab stopped.
His hand flashed in one smooth slow motion—
palm up on the steering column shifting into park,
When he turned around I braced myself.
palm down on the meter's arm.

The meter stopped.
I pressed harder into the seat.
Welcome home, Lady ...
This ride's on me.

To Do:
Kelly Greico

Make his bed,
Raise the American flag,
Clean the family room,
Stop for groceries, his favorite; cornbread casserole.
Prepare dinner,
Double check flight schedules,
Put dinner in the oven,
Pick Kylie up from school at 3,
Drive to the airport, his arrival time is 4,

Let him light the fire,
Set another place at the table,
And don't forget the trees outside,
where we take the yellow ribbons down.

Who Knew [how to describe]
Holley Watts

WHO KNEW…

how to describe what we did in Vietnam.
The brochure said it was a
morale program for the able-bodied.

We staffed our centers
so the men could come in and enjoy
some coffee, Kool-Aid, conversation, card games,
variety shows, whatever we could organize.

On clubmobile we went to the men in the field
by helicopter, jimmy, jeep or six-by
to Fire Support Bases, Landing Zones,
field hospitals and base camps.

We traveled in pairs, like nuns, one of us said,
and used our programs to suspend their reality
Sometimes the word was, Charlie's coming tonight,
and we'd join them to fill sandbags.
As if we kept score we'd always ask,
Hi, How are ya? Where ya from?
for just a little while.
their connection to family, community…home,
with smiles, a good ear for regional accents and a quick wit.
My friend distilled this somewhat lengthy job description—
We were the face of the girl next door,
and we were armed

Oh, he said, a cheerleader.

The Gargantuan Muffin Beauty Contest
Julian Stannard

We were at the Edison Hotel on West 47th Street
for the annual muffin beauty contest,
I can't tell you how pumped up we were.
Time Square was having another psychotic judder.
The bellhop was all thumbs up: Sir, have a nice day
and get one *gratis*. All those avenues of doors
and the Hispanic chambermaid who couldn't speak English.
Spiderman was doing all that Spiderman shit
just to get a bird's eye view. Donna Summer
was almost dead and we were barely into spring.
I want to dance to Love to Love you Baby, I want to groan.
I've never seen so many high quality muffins.
If I wasn't a religious man, and maybe I wasn't
I would have said the muffins were walking on water:
I've never felt so half and half. Have you read the Bible?
The bellhop said: You ain't seen muffin yet.
They were drifting in from Queens, Brooklyn, Harlem,
The Bronx, Manhattan muffins too and that weird
cute coke-faced muffin who'd taken the subway
from Coney Island. If only I were a betting man,
but hey I am a betting man, it's Coney Island every time.
Lou Reed isn't getting any younger. Zappa said
Girl you thought he was a man but he was a muffin,
he hung around till you found he didn't know nuthin.
In the lobby Nina Simone was singing, I loves you Muffin
and in the restroom they piped in Mack the Knife:
Hey Sookie Taudry, Jenny Diver, Polly Peachum
and old Miss Lulu Brown. Muffin the Romance
was the biggest show in town. We were hurtling back
to the 1970s and sometimes the 1970s are almost
as good as the 1930s. I want my muffins to be ahistorical:
shit, just to say *ahistorical* makes me joyful.
I saw Leonard Cohen crooning with a couple
of octogenarian muffins and I'm telling you now
the lobby was pleasantly disturbing. You may find
yourself behind the wheel of a large automobile.
You may find yourself in another part of the world.
You may find yourself at the gargantuan muffin beauty contest

and you may ask yourself, Well, how did I get here?
Time Square was having another psychotic judder.
Love is in the air, it's in the whisper of the trees.
This is not America, this is the cover version:
sun, sex, sin, divine intervention, death and destruction,
welcome to The Sodom and Gomorrah Show.
All those white muffins trying to be black muffins!
Give us our daily muffin, save us from temptation.
Jimmy Buffet was singing, Why don't we get drunk
and screw? In Times Square the most beautiful muffins
in the world were hanging on a thousand screens.
Where are my singing Tibetan balls? Am I dead?

Leaving Elkton
Sara Robinson

I cried and then sighed at their graves
Deep in the earth in their private little chambers
I wondered if they heard me
I came through on my way west
Hardly recognized the town
         Empty streets and vacant lots
Old storefronts hang around
They have nowhere else to go

Drove past where I grew up
Glanced around the neighborhood
I don't know anyone here
Pressed for time—like I thought it mattered
I headed for the cemetery—it was only a short ... a short detour
A cemetery for a small town
My parents are there
There were spots reserved for them
But I passed on mine
No one thought I would return
So today I'm passing through

At the gravesites I say some words
Catching them up with my life
I guessed they'd want to know
But then I didn't expect any response

Back in the car—back on the road, I hear my mother say
        You come back soon now, you hear?
I see the sun due west in front of the car
If I speed up I might
Cross a state line before it sets
        Before I hear her say it again

enter the house: desert ode
J Indigo Eriksen

enter the house
painted across the horizon
already I feel the longing
to guide along
with frozen breath
shaman robe
and well-sharpened teeth

dusty footprints now
desert skin where once
flesh knew rivers

hands of copal memory,
little sisters and masa
hold instead
empty plastic
2-liters of dust

to guide along
my feet
my mother's dead body
to guide along
us
we
my sisters, and grandfathers,
father, holding grandmother's hand

coyote said "venga"
follow me, Chiquita
mythic landscape
now oily smear
horizon brushes fingertips
so close
to taste
to lick the greasy fingertips of
Mickey D
sting of ammonia in nostrils
now that's the Dream

and god bless
if she had made it
god bless
the rest, though—
now that's history

the silent margins
her footsteps occupy
her space
the space where she was
a shadow

enter the house
mountains have moved
these are dry deserts
a changed skin
enter the house
in the third country
the country that exiled you
the country you went for

enter the house
of my hands
my dead mother's body

a dried out body
found by others
pushed past borders
arbitrary lines on a map
in the sand
between the words of
SB2010
NAFTA
CAFTA
just another economic plan

journeying soldiers
follow the season
tomato harvest
to strawberries

to another dream
visions of indentured servitude

call it capitalism
call it progress
call it western hegemonic discourse
enter the house enter
all hail the conquering heroes
in the land of plenty
plenty of stolen merchandise
genetically modified corn
floods the market
subsidized frijol for farmers
who can't afford to grow their own
because here we own
the land once known
before

when you couldn't buy a plant
I mean Forever,
I mean its genetic code
when you couldn't own the future
because who can buy a dream,
a hope, a vision?

enter the house enter
heavy climbing wind
dry desert
gnarled outcrops
of my father
old as a thousand hills
and my mother
old as a hundred rivers

and money is an invention
a system we create
because we buy into it
we buy those broken backs
that bridge they call
la frontera

we buy their deaths
for I-pods
playstation
the GAP
my laptop
your cell phone
National Security.
these clothes on my back?
Yeah, they killed her too.

Sweatshops on the border
So we can objectify ourselves
call it identity
call it fashion
call it just another way to stay on top

enter the house
of my hands
the house of forgetfulness
and see a girl
turning her face to the sky

and god bless
that girl-child in the desert
she left home
she got No Where
she died in our arms
as we tried to push her back
back to her homeland
no land
for her
the desert
now home

enter the heart
her heart
her house
the house of my mother's dead body
enter the house.

Author's Note: "Desert Ode" is a tribute to the following poems, all of which can be found in the anthology Language for a New Century *(Norton 2008) edited by Tina Chang, Nathalie Handal, and Ravi Shankar: "The Eastern Poem" by Gurbannazar Ezir; "Gondwana Rocks" by Dom Moraes; "In the Third Country" by G.S. Sharat Chandra; "Kabul Behind My Window" by Bashir Sakhawarz; "A Tale" by Salma Khadra Jayyusi; "This House, My Bones" by Elmaz Abinader.*

Letter to My Grandfather
Nicole Yurcaba

Dedushka,

Today I watched We the People
                         slit the American Constitution's throat
and smash Mother Liberty's face with the same sickle and hammer
which propelled you into America's arms 95 years ago.

Tell me, *Dedushka,* why We the People are so anxious to   throw
our liberties into dissolution. I wish you were here to tell   them
first-hand about starvation, assimilation, persecution
all in the name of "the collective."

I fear, *Dedushka,* that like you I shall someday be forced to flee
the land that I love.
             Tell me, where shall I go to escape the encroaching red,
which seemingly spills into Earth's every corner?
                         How can I escape the swinging
hammer of injustice, the sweeping sickle of death and enslavement?

As I grow older, *Dedushka,* I feel the sickle's singing blade
                         sweeping closer, closer, closer…

Author's Note: **Dedushka** *is the Ukrainian word for* **grandfather.**

Wandering Jew
Jacqueline Bishop

You take your songs, your stories, bits and pieces,
Of an unspoken tongue—

Once we were a prosperous family living in the hills
of Alegracias, Tarifa, Malaga and Granada; the men
of my family traded in silver, precious stones and one-of-a-kind
jewelry; the women made marvelous confectionery.
Our roots went deep. The tree of life grew strong.
From our homes high in the Sierra Nevada Mountains we looked out
at the heathen blue lands across the narrow passage of waters,
that Hercules, in his wisdom, used to separate
Europe from Africa. That was before the Inquisition
when we found ourselves running from one place to another,
that was before we found ourselves among all those other
flowers now growing in Morocco: blood red
hibiscuses, burnt orange bougainvilleas—
oh my daughter there was a soft mauve-colored plant
I haven't seen since that appeared first thing in the summer.
They say that for us Jews memory is our milk, our honey,
what we get our sustenance on, that we wished to turn
the beloved slopes of Jbel Dersa, the famed white dove
of Tetouan, into the long lost paradise of Andalusia:
and who is to say that they are wrong? When you have lived
in a place long enough, you come to feel a strange
attachment to the land. But then came violence, outrageous
taxes and marginalization in professions.
Though some of us would stay, most of us left again for:
Melilla, Gibraltar, Iran, Latin America—and here I am,
a tired old stone of a man, talking to you, his young and heavily
pregnant daughter, from the shores of a new and distant land.

Continental Drift
Lynn Martin

Androgynous defined
by a Connecticut ride,
you were that road
waif thumbing
with your back to traffic,
gliding from here to there,
driving time or better.

Sometimes you phone your mother.
Where are you?
She wants to know.

Dewdrenched on a foggy mountaintop,
West Virginia. Wake up!
Birdsong. Wind in the wild laurel.
Thumbing with your back to traffic,
once you turned around to find a hearse
ominous, waiting; and when the driver
saw your stunned, pale face,
he laughed. Then you laughed too
and took the ride.

Cattlemen and cropdusters.

In the desert, a sudden storm,
a vast violent sky
and you were afraid.

Tell them,
"I'm from the Bronx."
Tell them,
"I carry a knife and
know how to use it."

Hard riding independent truckers
tune into their CB radios,
high lonesome music,
and you to stay awake.

Cross country,
hauling to Baltimore,
but he took you to the Jersey Turnpike
Walt Whitman Rest Area
for just one
sweet kiss
on the lips
and that was all.

A breeze,
high dunes,
rabbits, coyote song,
star blast.

Where are you?
She wants to know.

John Elm
Apache warrior
Rattling Thunderbird
picked you up in Yuma
for a long beauty ride.
Scholars and sweating salesmen
with creeping hands.
A family says grace in a Winnebago.

Chicago rush hour roar.
The gust takes your hat
again and again until
you're weeping
this infernal evening
when like the wind,
no one stops.

Adirondack blizzard.
Kicked out of a squeaky rig
stacked tight with dynamite
because you had no interest

in the driver's intimate tattoos.
Snow swirl.
Soft snow bank.
Your lover so near.

How many miles to the moon and back?
With your back to traffic?
With your little songs?
With your frayed, green canvas
Boy Scout pack?

Pickup trucks with gun racks,
an ambulance, Cadillacs.

Stillness in motion.
Undulant transcendence.
Cracked cup of spat tobacco
sloshes beside you on the seat.

Coal miners, lobstermen,
drag queens, waitresses
all full of grace.
Kindness and grace.
Radiant transport!

Where are you?

Fable with Pekin Ducks
John Hoppenthaler

She and he were pleased that a brook ran through
their property, so they dredged and widened
and made of it a duck pond, which then cried out
for ducks, so they bought from a farm specializing
in such matters a pair of domesticated stock,

and though eggs were always laid, and what seemed
like thrashing duck sex sent white feathers flying,
the much-larger-than chicken eggs never hatched,
grew foul in their muddy nest, or they lay at pond's
bottom, turning gray as fist-sized stones. She began

collecting the delicious eggs and baked with them
her famous yellow sheet cakes and fudge brownies,
which she and her growingly detached husband
with problems of his own enjoyed with cold milk
or sweet tea on the veranda, which opened out from

their bedroom where sex was a problem. Country
life had done nothing for his ardor, and her clock was
ticking she kept announcing; *tick tick tick*, she'd chide,
tick tick tick. She dreamed of being taken from behind
on the settee, just inside the veranda's glass doors, crazy

sex from which a wild but beautiful child would issue,
and this miracle would so charm the fucking ducks,
she was sure, that they'd fight for their fucking eggs,
as well they fucking should, since life is so fragile, prone
to ill-use by the lord and lady of the fucking castle.

Out Here in the Country
for Dwayne
Nicole Yurcaba

Out here in the country,
in the backwoods,
in the boondocks,
in the sticks,
on Friday night
we do things a little differently:
ten-past-eight,
we pull on holed-in-the-knee Wranglers,
cracked-at-the-sole Georgia boots,
and grab our favorite Firebird fishin' pole,
and two Coleman lanterns
to hang from a bowin' tree limb;
we hunker down beside
an over-our-heads cattail cluster
at the pond's northern corner
and we single-hook
our nightcrawler dreams
to eight-pound test line
that's cast into murky oblivion;
we hum along to the bullfrog's song,
wishin' upon fiery lightnin' bugs,
conversin' with the barn owl
invisibly interrogatin' us.
Out here in the country,
in the backwoods,
in the boondocks,
in the sticks
on Friday night
we get our thrills differently:
when the orange-and-yellow bobber
drowns, we bend from our cross-legged sittin'
for our bowin'-to-the-water rods,
and flick-of-the-wrist set the hook,
reel-crankin', slow-fightin'
the freshwater beast
bendin' our favorite pole

nearly-to-breakin';
our cracked-at-the-sole Georgia boots
trapeze-line balancin'—muddied and leakin'—
the ankle-high rush-infested shoreline;
scamperin' beneath a lazy, yellow quarter moon,
 gleefully cryin' "Don't snap the line!",
"Just let it fight a little!" and "Reel in the slack!"
we pull the whale-of-a-catfish to shore,
where for a few unadulterated moments
the world on which our West Virginia's mapped
stands lantern-lit still,
revolving around us.

Carolina Handler
Lynn Martin

Sundays, I dance with the snake—
she coils in my arms and her
copper head, like a new penny,
weaves as I sway to the music.
And this is how I pray.
And this is how I pray.
Her warm long belly slides
knowing, now, another skin—not
rock or root or clay, but I
am as solid. I resonate.
Flick of the tongue and
she has my scent. We
were never strangers anyway.
We wind like the wild
grapevine—embracing Eden.
When eye to red-eye and
fearlessly we meet.
I am as teeming as
the spring-fed pond.
I am lighter than
a skipping stone.
I am a sacred woman—
a copper bangled woman.
My bracelets are alive.
And "I'm coming up.
I'm coming up on
the rough side of the mountain."
Here is the flame of tongue.
Again and again the tongue
stuttering as we writhe.
In another language I pray.
In another language I pray.

Then slowly ever so
slowly we uncoil and
holy Jesus on Sunday
evening sets us free.

Now, there are clouds on the mountains.
I stand where the earth is red.

Alabama Sunshine
John Lezcano

The Alabama sunshine is too far away,
it moves on as the day gets away
My heart pines for that summer day,
when all I wanted is for you to shine for me
I saw you in the Florida sky,
my you in a place where the pool was beside
Caught the first glimpse of your rays
when you looked with your brown eyes
And felt the heat on me when your smile blinded my eyes

The Alabama sunshine is so far away
That when I looked for you I had to search a ways
But you tanned my heart and I will never take that away
Memories are scabs that I pick at every day
Until the pain tells me I had my day in the sun

A day in the sun is just fine
A day in this Alabama sun was all mine
Now the Alabama sunshine has gone away
Night has dawned on my reality
I look for you but you can't speak
I'm giving my heart and all you can give is heat

I'm burning from you but I can't do nothing for you
You're so far away all I can do is adore you
Let me hold you, just one more time, smile at me till I'm blind
And you'll find there is love anytime whether day and nite
Cuz although we are two worlds away
We have a connection that I feel through me
Whether you feel that or not is what's concerning me
Where there's a will there's a way, well you got your Will
And I got my way,
a way to remember when the Alabama sunshine got away

New World Finches
Jacqueline Bishop

Everything happens little by little.
Everything is linked by one and the same example.
This is what Darwin believed.

Take, for example, these New World finches
that Darwin did not even bother labeling correctly.
These New World finches, all twelve or thirteen species,

Originating from one common South American ancestor.
Take, for example, their migratory flights from the mainland,
how they sing even while they are flying,

How they travel in small loose groups, these birds
so peculiar to the archipelago.
                        Take, for example, how individual groups
would populate individual islands,

their various adaptations—the shape of their beaks,
how they built the cup-shaped nests that would hold
the bright blue eggs of their young.

Take, for example, how these small dark birds
with their sad and haunting song, would, little by little,
become the great big link
                      in Darwin's explosive new theory of evolution.

Limbo
Dikson

He held a grudge against the Devil but more so with the God, pick one and give it a name ... he liked 'the great pretender,'

Sends shivers down his crooked spine when he thinks back to the time before the time before time,

When they were close,

Shared dreams like Yin and Yang tagged over with a smiley,

A delicate balance of beliefs snapped with the kind of divine carelessness that turns people into salt and runs blood through drainpipes,

The wishbone splintered halfway between the flames of hell and its smoke that billows in the sky,

The place where angels reside.

He used to be part of this holy trinity passing spliffs and prophecies around a round table slouched back in his chair,

Leaning on the weakest leg hoping that maybe he might fall and lighten the mood,

Let me introduce ... Limbo the clown,

He found deep pockets of inspiration in the lining of his hand-stitched, patchwork and polka dot baby-grow suit,

Colour was his thing, bright colour, slapdash face paint showed

how wide his lips would smile if they could,

And tears forming blue pearls in the place where eyelids touch hadn't met sadness,

Their creator was the unashamed joy that respawns itself in the split
seconds that make up 7 days ...

He knew not what they said about guys with big shoes scuffed
on sandy pilgrimages through time and space shepherding the essence
of his beliefs,

But his Technicolor crown birthed a burning bush of coiled
hair and gave him the idea to create Slinkys on the day that god rested,

It was the same day he made Dodo birds, dinosaurs, funny-
bones and wished the Irish good luck,

His breast pocket was where he kept his rainbows and confetti, ready to
add a splash of colour to dimly lit moments,

Baggy sleeves left room for his trickery to breathe through the
gills in his needlework,

And caution to the wind allowed the sun to give his nose a rosy
glow on the days he spent marveling at what his mother had
created ...

 ... Around the time we switched the letters A. and D. and B. and
C. and started counting numbers he was giving Jesus tips on
party tricks like turning water into wine and telling the Devil to play
dead to see if the world remembered how to say his name,

On days when preaching took place he'd burn effigies of

anything,
Dance like the possessed and speak human to human about

how some things are too big to describe so just trust your eyes and
whatever it is that makes you smile,

Scratching Against the Fabric

He'd carve animals out of stone and watch happily as carnival
kids walked around dragging these dusty figurines on the ground,

They were taught not to trust him but they didn't care,

He wore a smile while their parents looked to God for
punishment like masochistic children shaken by the
unpredictability of freedom and the fear of what death might bring,

For him, the blandness of purity and fables of the damned were too
tame a thought,

Heaven offered him only white and hell the deepest black but
he wanted colour because that's what he saw,

If this was a simple place where darkness stopped and daylight
began like twilight wasn't worth witnessing then he wouldn't
be here,

He wanted his story told but not in the scriptures by those who,
through divine pillow talk, birthed the ugly child he never saw,

No, he planted his spirit in painted faces and the diversity of
our fluorescent existence, so he keeps heaven and hell at an
arm's length,

Just close enough to humour himself with the fragility both and stay
safe in the knowledge

That the most high, with his head in the clouds and his inbred,

pyromaniac, red cousin with the horns haven't visited this place in a
long, long time,

And while the stitching in his patchwork might be fraying its
fabric won't fade, and his face paint is resistant to moments
when the heavens open,

He knows limbo doesn't exist between biblical lines but it's fine because
he chose to fall back from his chair flinging cream-filled pies as he did
towards the clouds landing face up on the ground,

Laughing uncontrollably at the irony of his banishment,

No longer would he be stuck in the middle of a chequered chessboard that entrances the colour-blind to believe

That in a place where life is as vivid as midnight rainbows

Anything could be as black and white as the time before the time before ... time.

Collapse of the Silver Bridge
m.e. jackson

She sparkled in the early morning sun
A jewel that spanned the ochred liquid way,
The hazardous Ohio's muddy flow.
Aluminum and steel suspended high.
Above the concrete pillars traffic passed
The busy life along route thirty-five.
Her soul was in the bedrock deep; her life
Held in the chains; an artery of trade,
A sign of things to come. A day for crowds
To shop then gaily head for home across
The silver span upon the fifteenth day,
A cold December nineteen sixty-seven.

No one imagined in the pouring rain
Of Cornstalk's hand upon the eye bar's pin.
A crack, a slip, and then a sonic boom.
The western deck began to fold and bend.
It shuddered, dipped, released its heavy load
That tumbled down toward an icy grave.
The twisting towers crumpled soaring down
While bodies mixed with Christmas gifts and bobbed
Like ghostly heads. A curse or flawed design?
That met with fate to meld within our minds
The memories of superstitious times.

The Meaning of Melanin
Kate Lahey

Tangled toes and lips
Slip beneath the covers
And the colour of our skin
Doesn't seem to hover where we are
Because we are veins and muscles,
the pulses in our chests.
Words like *black* and *white*
Are made-up pests, put to rest
As we tie ourselves in multicoloured knots.

History rots and falls into the ocean of our memories:
The seas between our ancestors.
Colonizers are colonized—we have all been raped and pillaged,
Land claimed and revised.
So colonize my heart.
We aren't worlds apart
We're the same.
No shame or blame
For the meaning of melanin.

Do you remember the ocean?
Do you have memories of hot suns
And sweet sand between your hands?
The way I have memories of freezing stones,
                                  moors and seas cold as bone?

I understand what I see,
But what I can't see
I can't understand.
Just as you will never know what it means to be me,
I'll never know how it feels to want to be free
From that rusting cage of history
The mystery of racism that seems
To elude our hearts
When we start binding our minds and find that its illusory.
Cursory fables of time long gone.
But I could be wrong.

Scratching Against the Fabric

While so many praise abolition and Martin Luther King
The notes of plantations,
White incantations
Still ring in the stifling air of political correctness

That looms like a black veil over tangled tresses.
Pretending like we are equal,
Hating differences that could be beautiful:
This is just a sequel
In which racial profiling isn't seen as real
Just disregarded as another rap lyric.
Where miscegenation is no longer a crime
But will cost you a moral dime in the eyes of the others.

Mothers, sisters, brothers
But we aren't.
Because when I hold his hand
You call me a bitch,
A snitch to your cause.
Essence magazine writing about how white women steal black men,
As if you are animals to be passed and traded in pens.
How, I can't understand the historical bond
Between black men and women,
That, I can never belong,
Be fond of him the way
You can.

But six black men in the middle of the night,
Trying to start a fight, saying that it isn't right because
You're a chichi girl.
Hits me like a bolt of lightening so frightening
My veins are screaming thoughts teeming "bloody murder"
But my tongue won't move,
Can't prove that they are wrong,
That I don't need their approval to belong.

Because we are stronger.
Not as some "interracial relationship" that statistically
                                                  won't last as long,
But as two giddy teenagers walking in a realm
Where there is no colour or structure to puncture our identities,

To make us feel like we need to defend some sort of legitimacy.
Because love will set you free
From bitches babbling behind your back
And the clattering clang of the word "chichi."

He and me and me and him
Are purple and pink and red and green.
We are the blue sky, the golden sun
We are dew drops on the grass,
The pink sunsets past.
We are the sands of Trinidad and
We are the green hills of Newfoundland.
We are unwound, unbound by words.
We are a shattered reflection of the past,

Mercury dripping between shards.

Memories and moments of history that we can disregard,
Because when we are tied up in those monochrome knots
Thoughts of forefathers and racist plots of past kin don't matter
Because we are in a place
Where there is no meaning to melanin.

Hopscotch Pedigree
Annmarie Lockhart

That's your mom?
Yes, that's our mom.
But she's white. How can she be your mom?
Duh. We're biracial.

One rolls her eyes and the other shakes her head as the darker two of
my three girls skip off into a new conversation with the other girls,
other girls a shade or two or three
darker than they are, they are
everything other and everything not:
tiny, skinny, athletic, studious in
their glasses, fierce with muscles and jab, cross, round kick
combinations, two girls in a group of girls,
fitting in and standing out
both at the same time.

Are they twins?
Are they yours?
Are they all yours?

As if the act of walking in the world is an invitation
to be interrogated,
as if coexistence is contingent upon passing an oral exam. Now that they
are older, my girls get the questions
and their insouciant answers render the asking meaningless. They all go
back to jump ropes and hand claps,
songs and dances, the chattering girl talk
of a playground of 12-year-olds who still believe
everything is just that simple, just that arduous,
just that black and white.

Hudson County Girl
Julie Ellinger Hunt

I used to live right across the river
on the New Jersey side—
Manhattan and Guttenberg like kissing
cousins,
West New York, a close sentimental lover.

I'd walk the line on the exaggerated cliffs
on my own,
the loner I fought to be
while pretty girls tend to have a small following.
Notebook always in hand—

I'd write gibberish high school woes
that seemed immensely important
to a fifteen-year-old always moving,
always trying to keep outsiders at
arm's length.

It was near that river
I fell apart and scattered all around
Hudson County
then healed
then fell apart again …

the standard cycle of a typical
American teenager trying to make
sense of herself and the enormous
world that awaited.

Millennium Retribution in Key West
Mark Fitzgerald

I

Ten centuries in the ricochet,
    a speck in the hourglass,
        dot of rain,
      retread,
      void.

We deserve this failure. Nothing stopped.
    What was is
      what is
        is what
          will be.

II

Damp first light, small
    through the blinds.
      Paper hats,
    half empty tumblers,
      discarded whistles,
        horns.

The world did not end. Nothing is not now
      how it's always
    been. Time, even in our
    time, is not our
      measure.

III

Nothing ticking
   except the memory
of Mallory Square: drinks
   on the wharf,
              the circus
speeding up—jugglers, ropewalkers, boats
casting off, gulls on the surge, salt on the gulp,
              the Gulf,
a turquoise window, a sunset tequila. Toss it back—
   some of the best moments
begin without caring
              —bite into the lemon.

IV

What novelty in sameness.
   How many others have come
hoping to dance,
              searching
for a vein to place their fingers on?
   A fresh glimpse
     at the continuum?
                Emptiness too
is a kind of fullness. The night gave
   more than it took. Soon I will head north
and see frost on the grass.
                Knowing nothing,
     I'll know nothing is missing.

Somewhere in New Mexico
Julie Ellinger Hunt

Like a parallel universe, somewhere in New Mexico,
a dust storm carries me back to you.
Floating fragments. Falling pieces.
Broken and beautiful.

The sun already set,
leaving an orange line across the cold ground.
A jackrabbit nibbles on his foot then sprints
behind a rock in lieu of the snake's return.

I'm somewhere in the sand. Half naked to only you.
Exposed flesh to only your eyes . . .
I'm somewhere next to you but nowhere you will see me
as the New Mexican heat gives way.

Out of sight, animals call to one another,
warning of night fears
predatory creatures that can see where they are blind.

I am blind too.

Blind to why you walk onward as I stand still.
Blind to your obvious flaws that should make me let go.
Yet I stand in the sand,
brazen to the dust storm,
always broken,
often beautiful.

Fallen pieces falling forward as you turn back,
only briefly.

Big-Rig Through Stolen Night
Mark Fitzgerald

All night the truck trucks
through the desert, a scene
so familiar as to become
unseen, all 18-wheels
barreling across wasteland,
time sedated but still on
schedule, a look of abandonment
through the windshield, it's all
headlights and highway, cash
on delivery, dropping
off, picking up, all 50
tons of it, tier upon tier, rising
and falling with clammy
palms on the wheel, a dusty
boot to the pedal,
the passage of sleep
in motion—who is it who shakes
in the night, shakes
on the road, shakes through the weather?—
with gears cranking
forward, shifting
back, boxes strapped
to walls, the truck
knocking against darkness,
deflation, desertion,
until the driver
rolls down the window
and comes alive
to the smell of diesel
amid green pastures,
the first sign of light.

The Wolf at the Door
m.e. jackson

She got out of the car in the
handicapped marked space.
A little overweight and limping
with few wrinkles and no gray hair.
How dare she park there!

She politely listened
to the stories of chemo,
radiation, and sometimes death.
They were healed, living, talking,
gathering sympathy and empathy.

She listened politely
but did not share.
No support group, no empathy.
She had her breasts;
alive but not living.

Only twenty-five and a young mother.
Petechiae scatter across her
breasts, legs, arms.
The first sign
of an early death if luck fails.

Morning stiffness at thirty,
body covered with psoriatic plaques,
light treatments every week,
pills that gag.
Trying to work and be a mother.

Thirty-five and finally a
diagnosis: Systemic lupus
Sun becomes the enemy.
Prednisone—maybe remission
but always the stiffness.

Life to live, but
intestines writhe in protest;
eating and sleeping a challenge,
ordinary chores a chore.
Children to nurture and love.

Fifty and a hysterectomy;
recovery takes months,
fibromyalgia attacks with
a sudden change of life.
Damaged heart needs surgery.

A shadow on the liver,
anemia, high blood pressure,
overweight and overwhelmed,
oxygen lost inside the lungs,
alone again.

She gets out of the car in the
handicapped parking space.
A little overweight and limping.
Few wrinkles and no gray hair.
How dare she park there.

Sixty-six and
barely living, but
she has both breasts.
She isn't sick.
Is she?

Guided by Stars and Glass
Annmarie Lockhart

In this place where lives
were risked, lost, and saved
in the name of freedom, this
railroad stop on the running
road, where a low whistle
ghosts the wind and voices,
a woman stands up and says
I'm pissed off.

On the radiation table
in the glass 6 inches above me
I saw my breast for the first
time, the bruising, the empty
space, the scar, the scar
reflected in the hard glare
the spotless glass, the
antiseptic distillation
of the new me

and I thought about all
the bodies that had lain
there before me and those
men sitting outside with
their prostate cancer
waiting for their turn
to be humiliated by
the glass.

I am charred meat,
FDA inspected,
an offering to the gods
in exchange for a mercy
that doctors and technicians
do not remember to show.

Voices around the room
speak of dehumanization.

These words resonate with
the echoes of hundreds
more, thousands more,
hounded by dogs and whips,
human property absconded
with by the theory of freedom
and the silent guidance of the
North Star.

Voices disembodied and intact
harmonize, sing the scales of
the soul, bearing its wounds
and scars, turning running blood
to rinsing water, cleansing evil
from branded, canvassed skin.

Set Adrift
Julie Ellinger Hunt

You deserted the island we shared,
uprooting it from beneath the ocean,
set adrift so I could remain unaccounted for—

I awoke to the angry sea letting go
and spewing out the bits you left behind
to remind me to do the dishes and feed the cat.

Above me, the sky that slowly turned before,
capsized until the sky was no longer,
and I was just a speck of sand beneath it
in the hands that used to be around my waist when we danced.

Set adrift, I write this as time must pass for you like before.
Never slowing down enough to plant your feet on steady ground
or gift a good night kiss on the back of a deserving hand.

Failed Romance
Stan Galloway

The little boy offers his best fire truck
and invites her to the box
while she sees the castles that he
has not built and the prince who
has not ridden to the rescue.
He says he likes the way she shows the
ribbon in her hair, meaning he likes
the way she shows the ribbon in her hair,
while she hears the one-tenth
surface to a nine-tenths depth he
won't reveal.
He reaches out to tie the shoe
string that falls loose and she
begins to list the hundred other
broken things he's failed to see, thinking
love and entropy are opposites.
He drives his cars around her,
happy that she chose to squat with him
for a time, and she wonders
why he needs her there while
he does his own thing oblivious.
Then she begins to talk and talk and he
turns his ear to her and finally says,
again, he likes the ribbon and
she turns away and leaves the box
to the shallow boy
with the one-track mind.

Been Loving All My Life
Timothy Wisniewski

It's easy in preschool. And kindergarten, I guess.
You just look around and love; you walk
up to the cute little blonde, pigtails and ribbons
maybe and BAM! you just kiss her, talk
to her. It's real. You don't think, imagine women
like Scarlett Johansen or think she's less
than you deserve. Look in her baby blue eyes
and give her your fire-truck.
It's the most honest moment you'll ever have.

Elementary school toughens up the game.
There are rules you don't know you don't know;
learn by doing, gets confusing, frustrating
so you turn the game around, you go
past her like she's nothing, push a little lady
in the dirt 'cause love and hate feels all the same.
Unconscious shift, swinging away on monkey bars but still
trying to capture the flag like it matters, to her.

Middle school is all about awareness. You
see Harry Potter in theaters but really
what you see is Emma Watson, not Hermione.
Desire makes things hard, you get feely—
hands & hugs, she shrugs, eyes crying "try me"
and you know all of nothing to do.
Awkward probing tongues—ah, the young,
oblivious in the dark and it tastes right like Jolly Ranchers.

Things come together in high school nicely.
Swept up in the river of shivers
you might find the one you know, no doubt,
is The One. With her you quiver,
you see the future plainly laid out,
architect of desire, dreams shining knightly,
nightly. Everything fits and clicks, content
together and it will last forev—

awhile. Just a little while for the majority
who will abandon the love when
it inevitably becomes too hard.
The world grows easier, doors open
and you decide love isn't real, a farce
of juvenile delusion. Your priorities
shift, you change with, until you're holding out
for Scarlett, sleeping next to Megan or Beth.

After this the illusion shatters.
You realize no fixed "game" will work;
assuredly, other experts claim otherwise.
In mind, the image of the prince; in eyes, the jerk
who is everything and nothing like other guys.
But still, you see her like she's all that matters—
she's cold? Burn the world. Extend your hand-held-heart
and hope her eyes light up like the baby blues
when she accepted your fire-truck to play awhile.

for Imad
Toni Stuart

it is the uncertainty,
he said

it is the autumn,
she thinks.
green leaves turn brittle
brown through shades of ochre, orange
and fear

four o'clock darkness pulls mists of
unspoken words from mute mouths
and hearts rattle inside
      seemingly empty bodies rattling
inside seemingly bursting train carriages
empty of happiness and
hope

it is the uncertainty,
he said

it is the autumn,
she thinks.
green leaves turn brittle
brown through shades of ochre, orange
and fear

rivers wind rustles
the forgotten
within and
a heart rattles inside
your sunken skeleton

your sculptured silhouette
breaks free,
its nude screams pierce the
makeshift masterpieces
that turned

your purple music
banal

and as these voices
fall to
silence, their sound
turns to ash:
a waste of passion
black like onyx
that now lines your insides.
the absurd makes you wild

it is the autumn,
she thinks

come walk with me through this cold November grey
along the Southbank of our lives, and let the dusk
mist settle on the winter of our unknowing souls.

it is the uncertainty,
he said.

i know, she smiles,
i know.

Good Morning
Emelia Wade

Glistening in the morning light
Terror strikes the chasm within my chest
Flash of white and lick of the lips
Panic sets in place
Closer and closer with every move
Terror turns into curiosity
A soft bite, no skin penetrated
but
blood glistens in the morning light.

Wishing Tree, 6 June 1977
Darlene Anita Scott

His hair brushes my thigh; strokes
bright like citrus fruit flame orange red
I grab a handful.
Tidy our want to order.

Mama, the welfare lady, riot of
doubt mute between my fingers.

He's fine. And when he says
we're going to be, I believe.

I braid; he slicks in and out of promises.
Search sleep to see if they're real before
he gives them, sometimes, to
nights he can't get home.
Wear wounds and funk so we eat
good, make love good, *Baby*
he says
we found it all
husky-like I take

the gifts of the garden
lingering on his breath; hands bristle
against my belly rubbing
me like a wishing tree so he
can believe too.

The Last Night
Timothy Wisniewski

Last night I never would have known that we
once had something incredible, something
special that set us apart, that made me
believe in eternity and made my heart sing
songs of defiance at oceans and mountains—
things that dip their toes into infinity on a day
to day basis but couldn't possibly comprehend
the idea of us. Last night I struggled for words to say
and dwelled incessantly on the imminent end;
we went through the motions, bad actors, playing parts
but I couldn't downplay the downturn in my heart.
Nothing was right, nothing felt the same;
I finally came to terms with the idea of finality.

Last night we ordered dinner to share and I could
not even bring myself to eat; last night we stood
on the boundaries of a once beautiful thing, long game
of love and charm, devotion and fidelity,
but I lost. I can go no further and I cannot lie,
to myself, anymore.
I stared at that ad for the oh-
so-succulent snow crab legs, but the whole time I
just thought about how much I don't like crab legs
and I probably never will … but you do—like them—so
I asked you to tell me about them, anything to fill
the silence. You said they were good to eat.
You said they were good to eat but even still
they were a lot of work, a lot of effort for little meat.
A lot of effort. For little meat. I'm sure they taste
delicious. But as we walked to the car and you
kept talking, I slowly heard less and less of the words
you were actually saying. They disappeared
and so did you. And so did I. Or at least,
so did the boy who sat across from you on
that last night.

Carnival
Stan Galloway

    Why anyone would want
   (or make) a three-foot stuffed
  banana, I don't know,
  but you said, "Win that for me,"
 and I couldn't dis-
appoint—twenty-seven
tries it took, nine dollars
by the foot, but it was
 worth the smile that you
  wore for me, and it,
   for hours even when
    the carnival had closed
     its gates and we were snuggled
      into bed, all three.

Overheard at a Bar in NYC
Annmarie Lockhart

Who?
John L'Orange.
Don't know him.
Yes you do.
No I don't.
I'm telling you, you do.

Midtown, about 6:00 pm on a quiet Thursday night.
Just me, the bartender, Jim Beam, and these two suits
catching up on who, what, where, why, and when.

What about him then?
He died.
Shit. When?
Yesterday, or the day before.
What happened?
Well, the story's a little unclear. Either a heart attack on the subway or he got mauled by a pit bull.
WTF?!

Barman pours another round.

That sucks. But I'm telling you, I don't know him.
Jesus Christ. You do. Alright, think back. Eighth grade, the trip to DC, remember that?
Yes, I remember that.
He was in the room with Jimmy O, Tommy B, and Wilson.
No, that was me. I was in the room with those guys.
No you weren't.
Holy shit. Yes I was.
Alright, whatever. Remember the class play junior year?
Yeah. West Side Story.
Right. Well opening night, what's-her-name got drunk and John went on as Maria and the whole cast got suspended.

WTF? That was me!
It was not.
Yes it was!
Are you sure?
Yes I'm sure!

The barman is standing at the ready now. Round 3
is poured as round 2 is downed. Two women of
indeterminate age roll in and sit at the other side
of the bar. They're yapping like lap dogs; the
barman waves them off.

Alright, here, you have to remember this: he's the guy that took Susan
Donnelly to the prom and they both got caught naked in the bushes
outside the hall.
Oh my ever-loving God. THAT. WAS. ME.
No way.
Yes way.

A moment of silence. Misidentified suit gestures for
another round. Barman closes his mouth and obliges.

Shit. Well then who the hell is John L'Orange?
Like I said, I don't have any idea. But God bless
the poor son of a bitch. May he rest in peace.

The Harbor Inn
KC Bosch

Ken Stop, check it out, we need to have at least one in here.
The Harbor Inn. A place so small we would have missed it
if not for the drunken sailors by the door.
Happy hour 9 till 11 AM,
No food but Angel will order it in.
We weren't having food but we were in luck,
Angel was working the bar.
Ice cold beer, no bottles just cans.
Ordering a round we find it the cheapest place yet,
of stop number six or seven, I think.
Angel was funny and friendly
in a "don't fuck with me way"
The sign behind her said it all,
"I'm not fluent in Idiot, so please speak slowly."
She tells us that this is the oldest bar in Ocean City!
Ken talking up the regulars gets one to take our photo with Angel.
It took some doing as "Danny"
was trying to get us and bar signs all in the shot.
I'm "talking" actually listening to Mrs. Bee
as she tells me about the great flood.
Barksdale the cat drowned.
Barks would have been happy to live
as long as the story of his demise.
One beer became several,
then we head off, lots more bars to see.
The drunks are still hanging out on the porch,
can't stay inside if you can't afford a beer.
We find ourselves at the Inlet Bar and Grille
Laughing and talking with Tammy and Jenny
The conversation screeches to a stop
when they hear where we had been.
You went into the "Bloody Bucket"
people get killed there all the time!

That is the local name for the place.
Still not believing till they see the photo of us and Angel.
They have never been there but know all the stories.
We had and survived unscathed.
The worst injury for us this day involved Vodka,
at the Mug and Mullet (or mallet) and not till much later.

Night Vigil
Nicole Yurcaba

"... but now a more dismal and fitting day dawns, and a different race of creatures awakes to express the meaning of Nature there."
—*Thoreau*

Past midnight conversation
begins always with the same interrogating question:
softly hollered from above high,
cloaked in full moon's milk,
illuminated by flicker-flicker fireflies—
"Who?"
which on before-dawn's new breaking
becomes the land's most melancholic wondering
being asked to one unsatisfied dying-ember soul,
the unknown violating trespasser,
lurking the twilight's gone-gleaming
led by sword-wielding Orion,
haunted by your spreading death-knell wings
through Life's criss-crossed tangled woods-web
while again you maniacally-and-double beg
"Who? Who?"—

Who dares trespass, break boundary into
your darkened forested dominion,
arch-angelically you dwell?
Who falls prey to your graceful, missiled predator-swoop?
"Who? Who?"
you ask, wise and dominant,
from skeleton-branch perches,
your razored talons warrior-braced for war-flight
when the unsatisfied dying-ember soul,
the violating trespasser
aimlessly wanders into your farsighted godliness
answering, humbled with pitiful self-admittance,
"I don't know; I don't know."

Woman at the Auction House
Angela M. Carter

"I ain't givin' nothin' away, darlin'," she said
as she pressed her stub of red lipstick to her lips.
She turned her head to the side, while her shoulders
    still straight,
 "Don't look at me so sad, cause ain't nothing easy
    'bout me, shugga.
My skin may be sold but this here the real 'pensive stuff
ain't got no dolla' signs on it."
I did not believe her at the time,
Her eyes looked easily swayed.
Every time the door opened we could hear the auction men—
their voices boxing to be heard over another's,
In that land of musk and lust for things that may
    or may not work—
Where we weren't allowed—
child nor woman, nobody nor corner warmer,
So I never had hope that I would
grow a voice enough to enter those doors.
Even then I knew that although our purposes different,
our jobs are to wait for others to want us.
Some men can't stop hunting, even afta' they own
    tha' fur an' antlers—
Darlin' you'll know it one day …
and ya might be standin' somewhere like this telling
some little girl the same thing and she
givin' you that same look you givin' me.
You'll see—"these corners can give a woman less bruises
and more love than that out there."
A ledge, winda', through glass and floor—
we've all got our corners, shugga … even you.

Capote and Brando Talk Over Drinks
Sara Robinson

The bar is on the corner
of 5th and Nothing Else
they talk about
their favorite gins
and other booze
that killed their parents

But that's too droll
even by their standards
so they talk about
great movie lines
and miscast roles

Truman interrupts
an opinion of his beret
would be nice
he found it at a
Goodwill store

Marlon wonders
if his black sweater
makes him look fat
They laugh at themselves
order another drink
        (And)

talk about the weather
in Kansas and other
foreign locations such
as the prairie
cold this time of year

Grasses bitter and dry
under flawed breezes
held by their opinions
but that's the gin talking
they must not get

too carried away
with scenes they
do not create

In all directions
they look around
hold their hands
up to frame
the outside—
fitting what they can
into the box

Between sips both
agree not much
is likely to change
their forecast

World's First Blues
Stan Galloway

Noddin' a three-note out-o'-kilter hum
Swayin' left an' right, usin' thighs for a drum
        Cain knew he was alone.
Three days before, they'd sent him to the east
Couldn't comprehend that word *deceased*
        He sat each night makin' muffled drone,
        Each night makin' muffled drone,
Dronin' the world's first blues.
In the flicker of the firelight song
Feelin' still the weight of what he'd done wrong
        World's first blues.
Shiftin' his hips, still apayin' the toll
There weren't no thing called rock-n-roll
        Just the blues
Oozin' from a human soul
        The blues.
His voice was high like a tenor in pain
You woulda heard that man complain
        "Kilt a brother in a world that has no en'
        Got myself to blame, who woulda known
        Alone in a world without no frien'
        Aloneness that goes clean to the bone."
Crack sputter pop went his fingers on his thighs
Searchin' for a rhythm that might comprise
        The feel o' the blues
        What the gut has said
        The feel o' blues
        From the back o' the head
        The feel o' the blues
        Wishin' he was dead
The same ever' night, he sang to the moon
Same three notes in a wretched new tune,
An' he moved to the east in his shufflin' shoes
Each day the song settled a bit more to defuse
The weight of the world's first blues.

Listening Ears
Kelly Greico

She learned the word at the age of four,
as she observed the world through safety locked windows,
buckled in her car seat.

Her mother drove her to preschool,
to the grocery store, to the park—if she was a good girl.

Mom assumed she was occupied
as she bopped to Sesame Street cassettes,
So when truckers and need-for-speed racers
suddenly switched lanes,
a few foul slip-ups probably went unnoticed.

But it was the day Daddy came along for the ride,
The sun was out, and so were the speed demons,

One quickly darted in front of Mom's CRV—

Faster than the cars on the road,
Little Kelly did not repeat Elmo's chorus,
but instead proceeded to shout out—

Embarrassment made Mom's cheeks brighter
as she stared in the rear-view mirror,
The stunned looked on Father's face
quickly molded into a slightly angry one,
as the four-year-old proudly announced,
"Asshole!"

No Country for Young "I"
Sana Khalesi

Where I live
Avalanche rises from your sloshed leery eyes
And your hands
Are my warm woolen winter blanket
of 49-piece cloth
Where I live
Leaves are colored black forty-seven more colors and white
And night
is Grey Truth of your painted Toy
NO!
I'm not Yeats
Not Vladimir Lenin
Not Helen
Yet
You lead solo-battle of Troy
A rush through my body
and soul
Hush!
far off on your head
Nine-and-forty clouds in a semblance of Saint Petersburg die.

Invasion of the Body Snatchers
(Don Siegel, 1956)
Chad Trevitte

We, too, in our colonial enterprise
Only came to save a savage land
Already gone to seed. Across their skies
Our podcast therefore gave the green command:

Absorb the smog of each anthropic ill,
Distill unsullied air from this stagnation;
Redeem their tainted blood with chlorophyll,
And bring a reign of righteous respiration.

Yet all our tireless efforts to reclaim them
Were met with shrill McCarthyite dismay;
And even though our waxy coats became them,
We failed. So much for our *évolués*…

We'll wait a hundred years and try again;
Perhaps we'll get a warmer welcome then.

Teary Queene
Sana Khalesi

Turning placid pages
all just rust on white
rightly as if going through Elizabethan ages
no words
like non-vocal notes on Luigi Rubino
'Les Larmes D'Automne'
music on the smooth paper you know
You can't lay eyes on the lines
or spot
the re-thought of the sophisticated suffocating signs

What if you could
spill into my thoughts
all outrageous
on the depthless doted-on pages
slumber
embrace or at least
leave a trace?

I descry a footfall
or is it just a zephyr
blowing in December
or through full Fall
turning to a beating blizzard
to concuss
to corral my name,
fourfold syllabary
contriving a mess in my head
in my hyperacusive hollow head

I feel incapable of filling it
fooling it to
outflank this anxiety attack and
track and
carry back your neglected pneuma and
rise and

forge
a fairy tale or a fiction
that desperately fits the diction of
your far-afield flinty eyes.

If my veins are full of ravenous rhymes,
if holding you tight is wrong
I shall compile a railroad
of sleek and still lines upon lines
I shall follow the tracks
I shall write
'you and I' as modus vivendi and
rewrite and
end in the magnum opus:
'One thousand and one you-less nights'

Stranger
Emelia Wade

Who are you?
Shadow walking towards me,
a man
Known once upon a time,
a prince
that was a warlock in disguise
casting spells on a damsel
NOT in distress
but curious for adventure

A Snap of a twig

He is closer now
but the story fades away
Lost
Buried beneath the sand in a magic lamp
in a faraway land
Never to be discovered
Memories forgotten

Like a mirage
figment of my imagination
Distant although next to me
This stranger.

My Rappaccini's Daughter
Timothy Wisniewski

Gorgeous as a sunset, deadly beauty
bold, oh! Be my Rappaccini's daughter!
Exotic flower, shoot sweet scent through me,
Behold—passion like the sun, but hotter.
Fiend Queen of Hell, torment me in the night,
Give me your toxic heart, make me immune
with love you feel that you cannot requite—
I wake in anguish, face paler than moon.
I care not for the danger, with me sleep,
Tenderly bathe me, aromatic breath—
Oh love malignant, heart and life do keep,
My Rappaccini's daughter, mine in death.
Stroll through our toxic garden, poison tryst,
We hand in hand, we heart in heart, shall kiss.

Before and After
Mark Fitzgerald

The discussion on "The Lady with the Dog" had been a flop.

Exhausted, the professor plopped down at a back desk
and stared at the words he'd chalked on the board:
escape, desire, confusion, home.

It was late. Someone had left a leather glove on the desk
beside him. A torn umbrella leaned at an odd angle against

the far wall. Light rain pattered the windows.

Earlier, he talked vibrantly of turning points, seductive reefs
and orchards, second youths, the white Pomeranian dog.
He wondered how much longer

he could keep it up. One student had argued the dog meant
renewal in Yalta but regression

in Moscow. Another suggested it was guilt biting back.

Everyone had their own theory and bitter experience.
Gulls gliding predictable currents, he thought. He brushed away
a streak of chalk from his tweed

jacket and recalled a woman he cared about, a deep ambivalence
in walking away.

Abandoned at last, he imagined dying beneath a lone cypress

on a cliff not knowing what he had wanted. Dying of tuberculosis,
Chekhov came to Yalta to rekindle a spark, a single moment,
he wanted to believe. Surely tropical skies

had something to do with it too. For years the professor
saw the white Pomeranian as a guardian of rebirth.

Stroke its thick coat: salute the penultimate death.

It was a choice that gave each word a lifetime of its own:
home, confusion, desire, escape. The sequence hardly
mattered. He might have been happier

had he stayed. Happier right where he was now, only
different. Or just as he was; he never knew how

he was—and now? Even then, it felt impossible.

The moment was driven by an afterwards that never
came. What he longed for was all that came before.
The rain had stopped. For an hour or so,

he sat staring at the words, still as a statue. He imagined
a train steaming off to Moscow, its lights vanishing,

cool air on a quiet platform, grasshoppers chirping.

Rose M. Singer
Brandon Lamson

Sam says the women are harder to teach.
Harder than the male inmates
corralled daily into my room,
raging at reflections
in that mirror-less space,
Bison and Menace throwing
punches in the hallway
as guards hit body alarms
and I bear hug Bison from behind.
Harder than the day a female
counselor spoke to my class,
one of those Beckett says
won't let you refuse a cup of coffee,
and the guys in the front row
reached into their FUBU sweats
and pulled out their cocks,
automatons raging against the inferno.
Even harder than that, Sam insists.
We talk this way to survive.
I call on him to prove it.
One morning he got a call to sub
for a math teacher in Rose M. Singer,
a women's jail whose name suggests
a gentle convalescent for flappers
or former jazz greats.
Brought in handcuffed
and in leg shackles,
they were seated at desks
and given short pencils
without erasers, no means of correction,
just cross outs and do overs.
Sam wrote an algebra equation
on the board: $3X + 1 = 2Y$
and asked them to solve for X.
Two students began arguing
about the solution, no single
letter capable of standing
for the rage at what was missing,

and since neither had enough room
to swing, one reached
into her orange jumpsuit,
pulled a used tampon
from her vagina and slapped
the other woman across
the face with it, with X,
Defiant X, *solve that bitch*,
X lost on the linoleum floor,
sweet jelly roll done gone
and left this world of sin,
the substitute for slave names
and the letter etched over
the eyes of the dead.
X, which multiplied and signed
at the end of letters means love.

Shane
(George Stevens, 1953)
Chad Trevitte

If you can figure out my success on the screen, you're a better man than I.
—Alan Ladd, 1913-1964

Like other starstruck kids, he saw in you
A buckskinned father armed for his embrace;
And when your somber, aging choirboy's face
Revealed a smile, your stature only grew.

But once that nimble magic hand outdrew
Its black-clad nemesis, such fatal grace
Could never find a quiet resting place.
You left the boy behind. No doubt you knew

Your name could never last. Yet still the sound
Of his bewildered, unrelenting call
Hounded your tracks through years of aimless trade—

Until, weary with shaking hands, you found
In six sure shots of Scotch and Seconal
An ammunition fit for lads that fade.

Earth-Two Sonnet
Lesley Wheeler

A caped figure slips through an empty building, inked
   figment on the brink
of the place where General Lee, tired of fighting, swore
   to serve as president.
Books wait breathless in their boxes; renovation's
   imminent.
The blackboards ache like thunderclouds. Power trying
   to break.

At dinner, it's all doppelgangers and secret identities.
   Captain America's shield is the Marvel standard for durability,
he explains as our son lists mythic forces that might
   shatter its
flawlessness. Nova Heat from the Human Torch; Hulk's
   avocado fist.
Their mirror-faces glow. *Maybe Thor's hammer,* they agree.

May that hammer slam
this Earth-One heroine. Let her drop the shield, ride the
   bolt to a parallel dimension and learn
to be ordinary. Let the afternoon level its cosmic rays
   at my back, burn
the scar-shadow-stain of the last few years onto the
   linoleum,
sketching a record of the armor I recycle, the tights I now
   peel free.
Allowed to wrinkle; skip a meeting of the League; be
   indiscreet. Her perfection only legend now.
   Vibranium chip of history.

walt whitman: a tribute
J. Indigo Eriksen

1.
four legs like two
difference un-notable, going unnoticed his leg on mine
whose arm, which toes curled against whose shoulder and
the heart beat pulse pound throb of femoral artery
yours? mine? his? hers? theirs ours me mine yes
all of it mine and me and I because
this earth and that stone and there a river
are all me as much as you
and I wonder,
Mr. Whitman, (shall I call you Walt? very well then, Walt, Mr. Walt,
WW) I wonder, sir, what do you think of cornstalks
what song sing you of them, for them?
a thousand and one brothers, sisters, brethren
together, erect in the sunlight
rainstorm cloudy blue sky day
like your blades of grass
all the same
difference unknowable
all me, all you
all of themselves
and different, a thousand and one beings
sacred story a song of so many
originalities and ways of knowing all things united in knowing
no thing here together we—the stalks of corn and
grassy blades of the 'beautiful uncut hair of graves' and all
these legs and arms and bodies with their various sprouts of fur and
tassel and bending flexing hairs on flesh on muscle movement
pure and simple like grace like grass like
a field of planted corn stalks on a silent loud insect day of chirp
and call and the sing-sing-sing of tree top beetles
sing their song of themselves and ourselves and yourself and
yes oh yes yes yes
myself, too.

2.
Mr. Whitman, oh that's right, Walt. Walt, then.
Walt, I, too, heard America singing
heard, yes, past tense, not hear
I heard a loud song trembling in myth and legend and hope and
dream and then I heard the silence of the in between
I heard the Soul
once whole, now pieces, a jigsaw puzzle of what could have been
should have been never, ever was—Walt,
let's be honest, you walked out the door in giant steps unbounded
to know America
to sing of her
to write her Soul in verse that galloped along the page unhindered
you witnessed a Something that never existed
except, perhaps, perhaps, perhaps
inside the lines of your hand that gripped
pen and pushed it to page
that knew the beards of hard bodied laborers and loved
the skirts of prostitutes and laymen and all men and all women
united together you saw the sort of America
I should like to call home
in all its uglies and all it glories, combined in beauty, and united
you saw this, yes,
even though, and yes it's true, you were not a perfect Soul
I've read your lines and questioned your punctuation,
the words you used that I would never think to use
but the one quality you lacked and this America, our America,
is much too proud to claim
is judgment
you, good sir, loved America
without haste and without preamble and without wondering
what and who is right to love
you made her to sing, and you captured that song
And I, too, went out in leaps so giant I thought I would never touch
earth and I pondered the grass, the Soul,
the bridges across this continental, athletic, native place you sing of,
your America
and what I heard was

Scratching Against the Fabric

the clang and honk and shrill of progress
of silent ones and ohs accumulating in the already swollen
bank accounts held off shore
the thises and thats of who's wrong and who's right
the dull thud of holy books clamped shut,
the interpreted word a new gospel
that directs missiles and war ships and freighters of trash
collected off chipped sidewalk roads,
the wailing of sirens to untuck mother from child and send one,
but not the other, back across borders
artificial lines torn across your America
(did you know there were so many americas, Walt?)
the smell of diesel and blood and metal rusting
the shiny aluminum of a new sign for the same thing which is to say
a thousand and one ways to write
no,
not you,
not here
not that way, your way,
only one way
America's way
I saw the lines of your America
the ploughboys and carpenters and masons
the boatmen the hatter the young girl sewing
and the mother at work
I saw them, I listened
I heard
and I saw the soldiers
and the bankers and the teachers and the mechanics
and the tradesmen and the scholars, the poets, too,
the musicians, the almighty orator, the simple cabinetmaker,
the dairy farmer and the feed mill operator—I saw them all
I walked your long steps, Walt,
I longed for the melodious song you promised
and, oh Walt, I am so sorry,
I did not hear it.
I do not hear America singing.
I don't think we ever knew the song.

Baudelaire
Chad Trevitte

Whether the lure was marijuana, whiskey,
Or Penthouse Pets nuzzling me in my sleep,
I learned the rule of *just say no* would keep
My temple clean. So I sustained my prayers
With Welch's grape and meager wafer squares,
While shunning any richer taste of vice.
Although the food was bland, it seemed less risky;
I'd get my just desserts in paradise.

Yet even as I ate my Sunday crumbs,
I watched how others fared. Cruising the mall,
The girls next door pursued Rod Stewart's call:
Young hearts, be free tonight. Later I'd see them
Pregnant at church. So much for carpe diem.
Such was the choice that host had given me:
Avoid sweet things or pay the price that comes
From too much fun in Kingsport, Tennessee—

Or so the sermon went, until one day
I skimmed a moldy book. It seemed to be
The stuff of some perverse patisserie
Where every sin revived a stunted sense,
And even rot retained a succulence.
My French was weak, but with each bite I knew
That in this foreign tongue I'd found a way
To have my devil's cake and eat it too.

Valleys Breathe, Heaven & Earth Move Together
Julian Stannard

After three weeks of continuous grading
I couldn't stop myself from making comments
and giving out carefully weighted scores.
So after reading 'Wales Visitation' this is what I wrote:
Allen, impressed by your energy and drive:
no shortage of rhetorical bravura
though rather promiscuous with the apostrophe,
and frankly the last time I visited Wales
it was so wet that getting on my knees
would in all likelihood have given me the flu:
 'O, Great Wetness, O Mother!'
And may I suggest that future hikes in the country
would be easier if you trimmed your beard
or—maybe—removed it altogether:
 'I lay down mixing my beard with the wet hair
of the mountainside/ smelling the vagina-moist ground.'
At such moments you might have considered
easing your foot off the accelerator.
but the project to move heaven and earth together
was, nevertheless, commendable. Ginsberg: 69

Dead Poet in the Passenger Seat
Lesley Wheeler

Dickinson flickers beside me,
a sepia projection
in too few frames per second—
an analog broadcast, broken

as trees break light. Discrete, despite
the slant-rhyme of us. She's dazed
by the persistence of her signal,
but grows sharp as she plays

with the radio knobs. She asks how I dream
and conjure while I drive
this carriage at such shuddering speed.
Observes that I'm not alive

to the blurred show at the roadside—plunge
of hawk for carrion,
stems staggering under seed. She warns,
slow down. I carry on

about parallel routes, the map
I might have used. Her image
goes snowy, faintly doubled. I ask
if she regrets her fine-stitched

silences. Thinking of words, she slants
forward, as if against wind,

and wrings her hands. She says, *oh, yes,*
I do. Too many friends

were ghosts, or I a ghost to them.
But glancing at her eyes
just for one attentive moment,
I glimpse the no, joyous,

the banked-up fire of her bound-up hair.
Her dash protracts—each inky line
sizzles like a telephone wire.
Connected the old way. Alone.

Pilgrimage
W.F. Lantry

What are the holy cities of America?
—John Berryman

There are no blackbirds on the Stevens walk.
We circle, looking for a seemly place
to park, and try The Hartford's spacious lot.
The young attendant greets us, but he's got
no notion who the poet was. His face
is buoyant with new generosity:

parking's on him. Our curiosity
drives us to find the rough commencement stone
set in this lawn along Asylum Road.
She reads, and I explain to James the code
engraved into the polished face. He's known
as a good finder, and he spots the next

just north. The devotees of Malcolm X
are handing out their Final Call, and stare
as I explain the third. A river birch
papers its bark before the red doored church.
I love the fifth. Its sounds, in empty air,
presage our storm. We cross the Brahmin Stream

to gated lions, once held in esteem
but fallen now, twisted by wind and snow:
the mansions have been sold. White faces peer
from windows, dialing. Silly, I revere
the last. A squad car watches as we go
towards the park, along the cedared block

Scholarship Girl, 1953
Lesley Wheeler

The scholarship girl paces to school
along broken pavements.
No one has cleaned up the war yet.
I swing my Shakespeare
against the wool on my hip,
my homemade blues.
Because I am tall,
I will play Caesar.

I will be smaller when I grow up.
Cockroaches will do their part.
I will study nursing
and go down to the laundry at night.
First I will tip the door open,
then stretch to reach the chain.
The light will reflect from a thousand
shiny carapaces scuttling away,
shrinking like a skirt in hot water,
lines forgotten suddenly.

But first there are rationed eggs,
and my sister calling *elephant eyes*,
and scholarship girls quarantined
in one crowded classroom.
Caesar's speeches will deflate
me one hot puff at a time
till I fit in anybody's pocket:
the starchy white one of the Sister
who docks my bus fare
in fine for laddered stockings,
or even yours. Listen
for my nails scratching
against the fabric.

A Room of One's Own
Kate Lahey

Caught and tangled in a woman's body,
Wrangled by the expectation
Of their glances on the subway.
Their moulding desires left over from high school dances
And prepubescent missed chances.
Yet still I feel like prancing in and out
Of red lips, swaying hips and blips of come hither glances.

Romances occupy my mind,
Grinding in my moments of being,
All else fleeing from my teasing eyes
Until I feel like I am lost—
Built upon materialistic lies of a vanity I am supposed to feel.
But the values which I hold myself up against
Reveal themselves as distractions,
Sexual attractions of a violent faction
Dragging me into a silent room,
Not of my own,
But built by another.
It's filled with mirrors
Reflecting all my fears between his walls,
Forcing me to fall into narcissism,
Rather than contemplating the fading thoughts
                              that were seizing my mind
Before the bind of their gaze on the subway.
They left me in a haze,
A maze I feel I put myself in.
Would my mind be brighter,
My thoughts tighter if the might of your eyes didn't weigh on me,
Forcing me to disguise my potential to even myself?

My mind a sacrifice for the body,
Rotting on the altar of your desires,
I falter beneath the sight.
I struggle to fight against beauty,
Wanting to bury my body beneath the rubble
So that my mind can bubble forth.

Scratching Against the Fabric

I don't want to be seen,
I want to be heard.
Even when you try to listen,
Your eyes glisten, pupils bristling, optically whistling

At the figure before you.
I desire to unlock my woman manliness and caress my naked mind,
To search within my womb and find Shakespeare's sister.
Yet I find myself scorning her, mourning her
Because I don't know how to let her out—
I doubt that I can escape the grout built up between these walls.

I want a room of my own,
I want a body not shown to the world,
A place where my mind can unfurl,
Not sleep curled beneath the omnipotent hum of first impressions
And physical digressions.
I want a room of my own built on the bones of Beadles,
Beneath a sky where cats float up to heaven.

Fire Builder
Jacqueline Bishop

I am by nature a conflagration—
I am by nature the gale force wind
that blows these mountains brown and bare—

Some say that I have become a symbol to my people.

I am the salt ponds of Sualouiga;
The if-you-could-only-name-those-shades-of-blue-waters;
The woman who can simultaneously see
what is before and beyond me.

We must unpack
The book of symbols.

Call me ill-tempered;
Call me bad-tempered;

Call me all-for-myself;
Call me all-for-my-people;

Call me the one who is always building a fire—

The names really aren't that important.

I am the woman in the bright red dress
Looking like a flamboyant tree walking down Front Street;

The woman who is always ahead of you—
The woman whose face you cannot see.

Call me Circe; call me Sycorax;
I am the puzzle; the mystery; the riddle;
I can become anything you want me to be.

Scratching Against the Fabric

Call me the mother of the July people;
Call me the July people—
All those hands raised into fists,
Holding that blood-red flower.

Call me mythmaker;
Call me Firebuilder;
Call me One-Tete-Lokay.

The (Poe)t
John Lezcano

Edgar Allan Poe flow my heart is a gothic gargoyle
The Raven says nevermore shall I dwell in this haven
Cut the pieces of me because my vulture eye tells tales
Under the wood yeah God does the saving
I was born into sin, I'm gonna die with a win
The Pit and the Pendulum how I take out Jew call it Spanish Inquisition

No prescription, I will not be drug out like Poe
For I do not wanna have a tragic play with a Conquering Worm
No need to walk life between life and death for that's a dream land
Although a year ago I saw death like El Dorado
Was desperado found an abogado who bailed me out of that trial
I called on the Lord, had him on speed dial
My dream was within a dream, some say that's inception
Yet I translated it to the beginning of a hard knock life
So this one's for Annie but in the end I finish these poems
Like Poe did with Annabel Lee

Leave this stage like her tomb by the side of the sea.

Poetic Vision
m.e. jackson

O Poe, I honor thee with thy
quill in hand
writing words so grandiose my
mind fails to understand.
In the darkness of your intellect
come forth the fears of all;
beating hearts and rapping sounds
maelstroms and a raven's call.

The thunderous throbbing in my ears
prevails in pendulous rage
as my eyes ponder the lines
etched darkly on the page.
I hear the tell-tale heart,
I touch the slimy stones,
as midnight ushers in
a black and lurid tome.

Save me from this terror
you weave incessantly
a shroud enveloping my being
a sepulcher of depravity.
But then I remember
romance infused your reverie
and left you loving lovelies
in prose and poetry.

As nightmares and dreams
slowly disappear
the sun gently rises
and erases all my fear.
Yet I feel your dread
and sense you growing cold,
imagining your lifeless form
and lost stories never told.

Julian, in Her Cell: 1405
Sarah Kennedy

Streaks of a cloud, a strange occluded sun—
omen for the storm by evening. I should summon
my scribe: the day leans already from its height

and yet my mind's sight is deviled
by the image of a king—how leaderly
he acts. I see him playing the religious

man, called by God to do battle. Bishops
at his flanks and France named once again
the enemy. He performs it well, but

my memory runs to Herod and the murmur
of usurper reaches even my lonely door.
Shall we have another year of war? The age

of emperor ruled long in Rome—it is written:
when statesmen looked to Olympus
for their crowns, the cities beneath them

burned. I must rise from this window,
turn again to my script, but the sky
darkens as I watch. Look how the swallows

swirl—an illumination, a book of hours,
a rumor of invasion in their wings.
But this is no era of prophecy, no time

of vision, no day to give advice to those
who grieve or fear or love. The world's word says
render unto Caesar what is God's, says sin

lives within resistance to power, says silence
is the sign of all true subjects. Do not be
deceived: the devil appeared to me

in smoke and fire, and as I watched, breathed
a pageant into being: wealthy men
and their sons of wealth, in rich, dark suits

of office. I saw autumn in their eyes, and hell,
and, look, now it begins to rain, just as

the birds forecast, just as the sun promised.

The boy in the garden is casting a sour look
at heaven, just as the traveling players
once did, to foretell a tragic future.

The Cellar Door
Lamaline, 1941
Kate Lahey

help your father bring in the sheep
she said across the mossy marshes
speckled with amber bakeapples
sprouting through the cold moor wind

his small feet slipped in the muddy prints of his father
as they made their way through brush & pine
somewhere on the sinking path
the boy went missing
among shrouds of salt and fog

he reappeared in front of the swollen warmth of the fireplace
his muddy galoshes smeared across the foot
of the only couch in the small salt box house
he lay calm and silent
next to the crashing waves below
as blood and globules of matter dripped
down his pale, hairless chin

the old salt stained cellar door
which had been sleeping amongst the racks
they salted cod upon
had been brought in earlier by the boy
and leaned against the wooden wall
to be nailed firmly against
a small box frame as the lid of his coffin

Disappearance, 26 July 1977
Darlene Anita Scott

A shoe.
Must have fallen in flight.
No matter now.
Come on, they're waiting.

"I am looking for my wife, my children.
She took all my children with her."

I'll secure you all, tuck you
into the fold
between these breasts.

I seep into the search after my shift.
My face a distorted stain
of sweat on the couch cushion
rimless like molten lava heaving:
"My children had no choice. They deserve a choice."

Mamas inspect
babies curly-cued in cribs
between kneading cassava dough
into bread and
windless with the work of answers
prepare bottles, hum.
We do not wait in our need; we make math of it
then solve the equation.

"Please don't let my children be your cash mortgage to Earth;
miss them more than the oranges of my nana's ambrosia,"

less than the sleep between night and service.

The Changeling
Sarah Kennedy

Testimony of Johanna Kennedy Burke at the trial of Michael Cleary for the murder of
his wife, Bridget Boland Cleary, 1895

Are you a witch, are you a fairy, / Or are you the wife of Michael Cleary?
Schoolyard rhyme, County Tipperary

Picture her now, no sheehoguey thing
spirited from the mountain by fairies
to cough and curse down her husband's house.

But neither my cousin Bridget. One
gold earring still in place, black stockings
on her charred legs, the rest a burned sack

of meat and bones. I never liked her,
I admit. Dress-proud. She made herself
the word on every gossip's tongue but

even I could see that a chest cold
does not mark a woman for murder
unless that drunk Jack Dunne is called in,

and what did Michael expect from him,
a fairy doctor, but "That is not
Bridget Boland"? I think of her now,

the fevered face, her fear when she pulled
me down on the pillow to whisper,
"He's making a changeling of me." I

saw only tuberculosis, blood
on her mouth, and if her husband was
brutal, well, I saw only the bed

she had made and would have to lie in.
Forgive me, I was asleep when he

doused her with the paraffin, I should

have seen it would come to that, the fire
was in his hand by the time I waked.
A chemise catches quick, and he was

mad, I could see it in him, belief
that she'd return as she was before,
healthy and strong, from some place under

the hillside, though to look at him here
you'd never think he was anything
but a space of silence. I study

the shadow of Slievenamon even
now from the window of my kitchen.
One day, it's a graveyard, dark, the haunt

of ghosts, gypsies, the Fenian knights,
and then it is nothing, a green bank
of cornfields, mirror of passing clouds.

After Sandy Hook
Lynn Martin

Take heart. Take heart, you workers
in the furrowed fields of love.
Try to trade bad thoughts for good.
Try to recall summer's creek side birdsong.
What a heavenly racket in that thicket—
a boisterous chorus, like twenty children at play.

Take heart. Take heart, all you workers.

Notes from a Rhenish Mission: 20
Don Maclennan

'The Mediterranean near Antibes'
is a slice of pale green sky
with puffy yellow clouds;
the sea itself is crazy, purple more than blue,
and into it is thrust a blade of cadmium yellow
burdened with flowers and marram grass.

There's not a person in sight,
yet this is one of Monet's
most passionate paintings.
If I am reincarnated
let it be in this.

Mannlicher Rackenakt
after a painting by Egon Schiele
Justin Walmsley

this man, in skin, needs no expression
mouth, shapeless, save for a slight curling of hair
burning by a candle wick, a hue of crimson and mango
his voice, like his bones and oil must cling to wrinkles
this portrait has both heat, ruin and sweat
Mannlicher Rackenakt has no face

environment without object, without face
the body remains the setting for expression
keeping from the naughty bit of sweat
between gaunt shoulders and thin armpit hair
feelings that are distraught and deep wrinkles
whose, in warmer light, seem fresh mango

this man, himself a dire sort—an infirm mango
revels in his starving individual and hidden face
the very acreage of which he came to find his wrinkles
how is it? he leans forward, hiding a seductive expression
tucking his head as if weighed down by bohemian hair
letting fall to his chest, or sheets, tiny loaves of sweat

for, what becomes of the naked model? but sweat!
a fragrance unknown to glass windows, scents of mango
products unknown to this tired individual with dusty hair
wearing nothing on his face
wearing nothing but our draconian expression
our convulsive wrinkles

so much more may be said of our wrinkles
the portrait remains canvas stained with sweat
who is this man devoid of expression?
his name is Mannlicher, yet might as well stand for mango
enough of him and his dainty body and fragile face
—he seems about to jump, his body is without hair

Scratching Against the Fabric

his legs are jagged, placed into his hips like to the skull: hair
each strand, fruits that are withered, smelling like wrinkles
his arms are extended and fade beyond his face
the frame seems to have been drenched in sweat
washing away the traces of darkened mango
his right foot, the sole, holds the greatest of expression

a man in bed—or not, naked and distorted, coated in sweat
resting on a sheet stretched out and weighed down by a mango
firmly pressed so that its spirit leaks into expression

Starship Tahiti
Brandon Lamson

I see Gauguin feverish and dreaming.

There is no cure unless casually accepting
death is one,
        the way Tahitian girls kneel
on the straw mat beside his bed.

I like to think angels falter,
occasionally turn their divine gaze
on satyrs who are tangling hooves below,
savoring the months of heaviness.

We want to mix immunity with the divine,
forgetting gods took the shape of animals to seduce us.

In Chinese opera everyone dies:
the man, the woman, and the other man
neutered down to a few gestures.

Before you finish undressing
let me change the light bulb,
        blue is better,
now this is our Antarctica,
our perpetual half-light in which nothing ends.

Clavicles steeped in blue shadow,
        above us stars
glow on my tapestry,
and if you look past either pole of us,
mouth or ass, there is a rip
in the ozone, a glimpse of afterlife.

how?
Toni Stuart

how do we
merge like a Dali painting
where eye is also
breast?
i want to feel you
as part of
me; feel your hand
pierce my side your
neck become my thigh but fear
sits here waits
for my desire
then
eats it.

Waist-deep in Sand
William Auten

All the cudgels in Spain
couldn't keep me from you.
Oh I am cunning,

a message finally delivered
on two rather than four legs,
a sportsman of sorts.

The good news is that private order
is like dropping the window-shade
on snow or covering a wound

with a longer-sleeved shirt.
Control of a personal climate.
Petite kingdom. Freedom to pick

the horses that will hunt the foxes.
The hawks and the falcons
you cannot have.

Murder of crows—yes.
Ravens, rooks—
all those with black wings.

We should chat
about the places
we've been.

There is overlap,
cities left to conquer,
flights to catch,

unexpected white sunsets
to press against.
Tell me something

Scratching Against the Fabric

I don't know.
Or show it to me,
where it grows blindingly,

slower, becoming level and full,
until it's unable to find
its breaking point.

Swim
Justin Walmsley

*

a word for those
concerning soul

this is not a song
i cannot speak

for sisters

their posture torn
cadence sore

facing sun, under
cool saffron

for purple

a word for those
       concerning white

skin, i have not yet
felt comforted

for those

without groove or toe
       people unconcerned

who, without ears
       feel only breath

against ear

who, without lips
       feel only teeth

Scratching Against the Fabric

this is not a song
        i cannot sing

against soul

*

We'll grow here. from off-centre, dear
like melody, which cannot be contained
or simply jotted down on music paper; only felt-like
smooth wool, humid and harmonious

take sight of these sagging willows
heat exhausted and colour of wheat
        stare honey! we are furious.
Water leaks and take shelter

under root and roofs of splinters
        our nectar flavour, so sweet
sipped through flutes and flames
        outer cities, whole grounds surrounded by a marsh

        where a gale of hummingbirds whisper
a lovely kind of afraid, pushing hair apart
        words deep into your ears like calligraphy on brick shivers
waves climb up from your toe to the nape of your neck

your heart dips
        and jigs
                smile darling until you sleep

and

swim

oh! you won't need rubber wings
                                          to breath under waves of string
follow our voice and African drums
                                              move a little; watch the surface
break
succumb to shore and siren vapors
                                    bath in salt and read our vines

swim

it's not, simply, us
        strong women and peach allure
with fine skin and eyes that quiver twigs
        voices as sharp as sugar crystals

        hair, nappy yet soft
always soft
        but men too, whose bodies are built strong
are just … fields and soil tended to by rain

We do not frolic through some garden like dazed and starving
        scavenger birds
picking to pieces stale bread or fruit pits
        we stroll and pause

wait

        continue strollin'
our flow like pollen and wispy weeds
        whistled by some woodcarver without spit
destined, on some buoy, to write a myth in timber
        of how he came to sing

      to be lured
           to our ocean
                forever

swim

oh! you won't need rubber wings
      to breath
                              to breath in savory tickle
empty stones from your heaving pocket
                                      you are lighter; we're no
vendor squeeze
drown. we're just splendor

and you!
you dance
underwater as if your spine had slipped

swim

*

… dedicated to eyes like hazel.

We'll pretend
           they'll hardly listen

so we sing!

on and on and stronger
                while your rhythm

stumbles

like smooth wool under
                bramble tension

sharp glances
                from pretty overcoats
                              hiding naked shoulders

Battery
William Auten

I used to wait
for the important features
to arrive. Mostly the days
would roll out possibilities
demanding full attention
from the skin. Other times
there was a looseness
akin to silk held between hands
trying to keep it from slipping
but sending it out just enough
so it could get under a machine
and come back beautiful
with wonderful patches
and stitches up and down the sleeves.

You may ask yourself
if important action is the only thing
needed in the unscripted dark
for such conceits—
that desire covers the world,
and you're tired of trying
to lift it and see it
as forgiven, that no promises
are left to keep,
that even the soothsayer
has picked up the bones
and head to the beach
for the rest of summer.

As for us, directions need grip,
teeth in the shallow tread,
but flour on the trail helps too:
turn here and then here
before intense heat
and an unforeseen cold-front collide,
dissolving both the place and your pace.

And water seems to play out differently
than you had hoped:
Are there any spirits left to conjure?

If blood absorbs an oath,
then I don't want to squeeze it out
onto whatever surface I could hold,
which would pose problems
for future generations—
like varnish on a painting
the painter did not intend.

But you want to hear from anything
that says There's more ahead,
but the peloton refuses
to break from itself
and slowly saturate its colors
into a river winding through the city.

Prick the thumbs, cross the fingers,
pin a note to the chest,
how is it exactly you will want
to remember transitions and unexpected stops?

During dessert, over cloudberry pudding,
days are preferred because crashing
into large vestibules of moonlight
won't separate them right away.
Protestors seem to understand this
when first planting pinwheels
in the closely cropped lawns
of mega-corporations
then moving on to larger-scale
performances of civil disobedience
and continuous gestures
of welcoming strangers.

Scratching Against the Fabric

We get tied up perceiving
the immediate but minor results
bearing down on us at all hours;
but do you realize
such extraordinary small offerings
are dipped in the glow of late spring?

The to-do list remains connotative:
Paris, food, lights,
travels by foot alone
in other empires.
The taste remains the same
even though the atmospheric effects
would have us believe
that in a foreign scene
we turn differently to each other,
in pink-tinted weather,
if we will turn at all.

That illusion seems to be
more pressing. Forget the on-cue
result of Pepper's ghost:
certainly the woman and the gorilla
were in the same box
but at different angles
and passed through
opposing shadows,
creating a wicked season
for the theatre.

Not all angels
have made themselves known;
if you agree to this,
start your answer
with the texture of sand.
Otherwise, earlier participants
will want to be accounted for,
a relighting of candles,
those who had houses in the village,
cleared paths from sea to woods,
but whose sleep has been disrupted.

They remind us of times
when diseases were char black,
started among the outcasts,
and ruptured the body
from the inside out
until it was clear
the great playwrights
weren't afraid to show us
a burning head,
with wide eyes,
and its owner,
whom we recognize,
wrapped in a grey shawl,
out in the cold
looking for us.

She wants to whisper
something so uncomplicated
that it can be easily opened
on a long ride home.

Anthem
Phillippa Yaa de Villiers

Words sketch images on the air.
Voice sets them on fire. I watch traditions
foot stamping, dancing themselves
back to divinity
singing that old song
that we all know as freedom
and a heavy flood bursts
through the chambers of my heart
bright red vital ...

I am alive:
my heart the same size as this fist and I
as little as this finger. We are all connected,
the living and the dead.
We arrive in life and then it
walks away from us;
leaving our bones behind
and our minds are as wide as the universe.
Human evolution began in this corner of the earth,
our ancestors left their dust as chromosomes
in each of us, they made a home,
and hominids stood up as humans and walked
languages fell out of our mouths and talked, walked their way
into and out of landscapes, mindscapes.
We walk in words, creating as we need:
we stand shadow-thin
and then
we chase the horizon disappearing
until we appear again.

Miracles exist. Victims become heroes:
a woman who could not walk swam to golden glory,
a man with no legs was the fastest runner in the world.
Our brains are two halves, reflecting duality,
a system of thinking
in pairs of opposites
like an on-off switch:

like a two way street:
day night wrong right man woman black white
Caster Semenya the talented athlete
was an invitation
to consider the end of two-way thinking. A provocation
asking us to refine our definition of what it means to be human
or woman. A conundrum. We find ourselves in a hard land
that we don't understand, we've never been here before but
this is what the future looks like. We will have to
stretch our minds from a street
to a field to an ocean to a universe to
accommodate our infinite uniqueness.

Miracles exist; we carve them out of our bodies,
we hammer them out of stone and copper,
we weave them out of desire:
for what the world does not contain
our minds create a home, as long as
we are alive,
our hearts as big as our fists and we
as little as our fingers. We are all connected
the living and the dead,
and our minds
are as wide
as the universe.

Buffeted
John Hoppenthaler

Stoned in the canned jangle of steel
drum tunes in the faux Tiki bar, I sit below
dusty plastic fronds and nurse my drink. A few stools
down, too precious for words, a tongue-studded, nose-ringed,
lesbian couple, heads bowed close, whisper secrets
    and softly laugh.
I want their love to last.

I order a plate of clams oreganato
with crusty French bread on the side for dipping
into the buttery broth that strongly hints at salty brine.
Ted slides another frozen margarita down the lacquered
surface of the bar top while some raw, tequilaed-up
    synapse fires,
and I remember the Paul Simon

song that mentions two fragile ex-lovers
speculating over who's been damaged the most.
Guess what?: I think of you: how much like the book
you said you could read me like this is of me: to flounder
still in our marred way of being together in the world.
    I love the dead,
dumb clack of emptied shells

as I assemble them into a stylized pile, as if
building an already weathered monument to sailors
the night sea took away and never gave back. Damaged
dreamboat. Damaged land. Damaged ocean. Damaged man.
Damaged woman. Damaged tide. Damaged moon.
    Damaged pride.
Damaged angel. Damaged wing.

Damaged Jesus. Damaged everything. I don't think
it will last, though the adorable lovers have now gathered
tightly in each other's arms and seem, in this
    heartbeat, defiantly
inextricable, their matching dragonfly tattoos
    now visible, poised

as if for trans-Atlantic flight on each girl's right
    shoulder blade. I
think of the artist's needle, how it broke the skin.

Metallica Burns on the Altar of the Viking Rockstar
Brandon Lamson

It was thrash in a steel town. Day jobs as night managers
tending an oracle
                of gasoline fires and industrial accidents.
Flaming suddenly into verse and chorus
they wanted to be poured into glass bottles and hurled.

This was their first album. Before detox.
Before therapy, forced to cut their hair and reflect.

The awkward postures of youth resemble
something molting,
                ripping through
a hairy pod and spitting goo
from its mandibles, waving its praying mantis limbs
in a strobe lit cloud of pheromones.

The first recording I ever made
was in the basement of my grandmother's house—

my friend Charlie and I told stories
                            into a tape player
describing the exploits of Vikings who pillaged
and fucked their way through southern Maryland.

I'd read many fantasy novels,
but I liked the cover illustrations
best, paintings of muscled heroes armed
with swords
        and women clothed in animal skins
kneeling or chained or thrown
over the hero's shoulder.

My friend, a foster kid, showed me the scars
on his stomach and legs from numerous skin grafts.
When he was an infant
                his mother dropped him

in boiling water or spilled it on him, accidentally
or not and he was taken
from her and raised by our neighbor,
a drunken army lieutenant.

I imagine him compelled to speak by an indescribable pain
inflicted on him before he knew words.

Our stories overlapped and entangled
as we recorded them,
      stopped and replayed the tape
to hear our voices.

Thrill of an exotic beast captured,
prowling the yard, the pattern
       of its striped coat shifting
as its muscles lengthened.
     Once the tape was found
my punishment was to listen
while my parents and grandparents blasted it
at the dining room table.

Dear elders, I'm still shaming you,
writing it down now so you can't erase the pulverizing drum.

Go ahead, you can taste
this paper lubricated with semen and bourbon;
it's flammable,
and your names may be written there, leaves
destined for a manual
on how to become a Viking Rockstar.

Well-Regulated Dumplings Are Going Upwards
Julian Stannard

They're playing jazz in the Platz
which is cool because when you smile
the whole world wants a little Schnitzel.

They might be old and melancholic
but they're playing jazz in the Platz
which is cool because when you smile
the whole world wants a little Kunst.

They're playing jazz in the Platz
which is cool because they're making
little rooms in your head which
are so light and so free

that Ludwig One and Ludwig Two are going into the air
that The Rathaus mit Glockenspiel are going into the air

that the Blumen and Schweinenacken are going into the air
that there's been a sighting of Max Beckmann up in the air

that the Englisher Garten are absolutely gorgeous in the air
that Rudolf Steiner has become a special rocket

that well-regulated dumplings are going upwards
that buckets of whipped cream are going, going into the air.

This is a lightness which is lighter than light
this is a lightness which is lighter than skin
that I have to ask myself, Can this be death?
but why wrap yourself up in knots about a thing like that
because when you smile—ja—because
when you smile the whole world smiles with you.

Domestic Garden
John Hoppenthaler

A ghost has disarranged these roses
    lining the walkway. Some greenhouse
        jokester must have switched

Jackson & Perkins packaging—*Heaven
    On Earth* for *Change of Heart, Black

Magic* with *Beloved*. I'll name them
    rancor lilies in your absence, though
        I don't hate you, & they're not lilies,

& you aren't really gone, except in the way
    presence sometimes contradicts itself.

Should they grow on me—fugitive varietals
    I never thought to plant—will they lure
        your bouquet any closer, spirit

away weeds I'll name neglect, aphids
    who'll stay aphids, sucking at the stalk?

Notes from a Rhenish Mission: 18
Don Maclennan

After the fire,
black ash streaked with white
palls the ground.
Bushes with raw burns
wave orange leaves
in mute distress.

Words only point
to the event, and fail.
Their meaning winces
in the rancid aftersmell.

I've Heard of You
John Lezcano

Put in the seat where Scarecrow judges me
San Andreas Faults destroy the homeland's horizon
The Reporter records the magnitude and casualties
A ghastly sight deafens your ears to the process
I've heard of you, Tinseltown with all the lights

Live in a world where if you slip up, they call you Judas
You go gaga and become the paparazzi
Weekly, the people read these tabloid headlines
The Days of Our Lives under a microscope
I've heard of you, cemented stars in your Walk of Fame

Many times the roses want to prick skin but they have no thorns
Never been in soil where they couldn't grow
See the root of problems comes from judging the petals
Pollinate the mind with whatever bumblebees want to do
I've heard of you, a rose who's known by the bricks

Chase these bricks to the border for bricks are kind killers
Bricks break bones with gentle answers
Bricks see more evil but assist with their ladders
But are we really just another brick in the wall?
A valley of silicon bricks?

One True Story
Sarah Kennedy

An astonished physician holds
a stethoscope to the bare chest

(four car bombs today on the news,
following the three yesterday)

of an ailing, ordinary
patient who is watching him work,

(the insurgents have died and now
the civilians wander, bleeding,

one twisted traffic sign is left)
who is silent at his warm core.

For the rest of the surgeon's life
he will say, over and over,

that the man gazed into his face
with seeing eyes, mouth opening

(nineteen dead today, then twenty,
now thirty-four more dead, hundreds

dead now thousands on our TVs),
the mouth speaking from a body

already absent its heartbeat,
already dead at the center,

the man always about to fall
into his arms (casualties

countless now, smoke storms from the flames),
the street outside, framed by window,

silent-seeming and painterly
in memory (an explosion:

origin nowhere, circumference
everywhere), the hollow voice,

the cells of the chords switching off,
saying, "Doctor, something is wrong."

Splinter
Angela M. Carter

I dream you back to take out a childhood splinter:
You say, "Look away if it hurts"—
Your wrinkled hands pushing the thinnest needle
into a cave the splinter built.
I adored the attention your fingers dedicated to mine,
And I prayed that you would find a trace of another thorn
lodged under the skin of my palm,
forever to be a puzzle you had to endeavor to solve.

I want to take back the moments of storm dorms
crying at the presence of a stranger,
When we lived for the rain to cool us and feed us all at once—
Days when men were only husbands and fathers—
Nights where a lover didn't rub the skin right off a women's
heart during their morning escape—
Mornings that I was not left alone to scrub my
disappointment off the wrinkled sheets.

If memory were to choose a body, it would be a woman's;
She would greet me in the cold hallway with a stuffed blanket.
Once I sleep, she would sweep me into small piles of grainy pain
within the corners of the room
and place the most comfortable chair atop of me
as the liquor bottles glisten in the windowsill.

I dream you back to take out a childhood splinter:
You say, "Look away if it hurts"—
In some ways you breathed easier when I turned
my teary eyes to the wall,
So that is what I'll forever do.

For K
Kelly Greico

We'll be old when we grow up,
But our friendship never grows old,
I predict our friend future
Will still contain daily jokes about Channing followed up
with a "That's What Makes You Beautiful," sing-a-long sesh.
I envision us, age 64, living as neighbors with matching front porches,
We'll rock out in rocking chairs to my girl Hannah Montana,
Maybe have grandkids of our own
as backup dancers for our performance.
BC will come up often,
Maybe we'll have buildings named after the legacy we left behind—
Your art work, my teaching career,
And roles in leading the alumni association,
Can we knit matching "EAGLES PRIDE" sweaters for football games?
Coolest grannies on campus,
Kickin' it *old school*,
Driving stylish Hybrids and bumpin,' back-in-the-day, Britney beats.
Honors House 420 may be gone, replaced by Stone Village expansion,
I wonder who, out of our current circle of friends, will still be friendly.
Who will we stay connected to?
A few may go on to be famous and rich.
Not *rich* the way we are of course.

How about husbands?
After dating such "lovely" boys,
I pray we find ourselves Men.

Forget worrying about being married now though
Too stressful, too soon, too much holding us back!
Let's enjoy trips into DC just to escape,
And let's go to Target more than the employees who work there.
Let's travel and get drunk over spring break—
but not the way girls do,
The way classy sassy women like us do—
With*out* embarrassing Facebook photos.
Let's paint our nails,
adding the one accent nail of a different color.

Scratching Against the Fabric

Let's go to the gym,
and treat ourselves to cookie skillets after.
Let's stay up late
just to watch *SNL* skits we'll quote tomorrow when we text.
And let's bake,
have facemasks night,
take hilarious Mac Photobooth pictures,
and plug-in our Christmas lights all year round.

Weekend nights bring wonderful adventures,
But side-splitting Saturday nights
quickly turn to Sunday mornings.

On Sundays we attend service together,
We leave church warmed up for the week ahead,

And with each prayer my heart whispers,
I thank God For K,
For friendship magnificent and pure.

Right now, we'll continue to vent about the upcoming semester
and the Honors House whiteboard reading: "475 days left!"
may leave us solemn when it reads: "1 day left."

Graduation Day,
Listening to Vitamin C,
Won't be the only reason we cry,

Between the mixed emotions,
The moments captured on tape, or stored in our souls,
We'll take everything we share,
And we'll grow,
Strong, beautifully, and *rich*.

We'll be old when we grow up …
But for now, We Are Young

For now, we'll keep dreaming together

heart beat
J. Indigo Eriksen

step one
open fist
allow palm to blossom
like a purple rose
growing from a dumpster

two
press palms to sky
and give thanks
today
no bullets
no dead stuff
no police
just … love

three
push palms into ribcage
break apart
stiff bones
press past tendons
muscles, connective tissue
and feel
heart
hot, thumping and pounding
and beating out a message

ba-bump
ba-bump
ba-bump

four
today grandmother's kitchen
full of biscuit smells
and big sisters
and big brothers
full of life
so new, so fresh

Scratching Against the Fabric

you can taste it
this life
fills your mouth
your stomach
your hands

five
today we close Pandora's box
they said we couldn't do it
but we did
put them all back
those hands that killed our family
that lynched brothers and sisters
that changed the name
of this
nuestra tierra
into another thing
today we put them back
and Death becomes a God
again

six
today
we will write no more letters
to a judge deaf to us
and blind
not like justice
just blind
on purpose
today
we write letters
to each other

seven
press palms together
a prayer
but we pray standing up
no broken backs
no bruised knees
no bones hitting pavement
not today

eight
today the trigger
does not work

nine
place hands into paint
all the colors
fingers covered in
black, red, orange, white, pink, green,
purple, and blue
this paint today
is something new
something for us

ten
press paint covered hands together
in prayer
we remember all of you
now gone
press paint covered hands together
in prayer
pushing palms into chest
find heart
beating heart
mother inhales, father exhales
we are born, these hands these hearts
cross your fingers
close your eyes
deep breath

new year coming
I greet you
with open arms.

Revisiting Past's Seasons
Angela M. Carter

I choose my soul blind
And use old drapes of memories
to mask the colors I select it not to see—The girl I was
taped my inhibitions on the outside panes of my bedroom window
and every once in awhile my nails scrape a fine tune across the glass
to try and reach them.
But that naïve tadpole, once inside, knew little of the raw meat that
hangs from a woman's ceiling
and drips on her white cotton sheets as she rests for the new day.

All the choices I made with greatest intentions
mean I can never be new;
the hands I choose to hold walking into a dark room,
the selectiveness we encourage when remembering …
and telling why we returned
when we wanted nothing more than to run away.

There is a realization that all this must seem quite sad,
But I relish the crevasses that dine on my skin—
And the nine months of belly that is from overeating trust,
Folds inside a body that houses aged senses.

No, we cannot ever be unseasoned.
It was only when I tossed my life like a rock
that I stopped chipping myself repeatedly like a delicate figurine.
Nothing can ever be restored to its nativity, but it may renew.

There may still be breath where the chest isn't seen rising
if pupils still adjust to the light.
There may still be a trauma where old blood has dried,
But, my God,
where there is a wound the blood knew the vessel was still alive!

God's Watermark
Cynthia Atkins

At the window, gazing up
to the essential heavens, my son asks,
"Is God Perfect?"—as if there were
a book to look it up. He understands
that God is larger than the kitchen,
larger than the outstretched land.
He comprehends Darwin, and numbers
so far flung our minds can no longer
arrange them. He knows *infinity*—
He knows our lives
are foregone conclusions.
   I can't begin to tell him
anything he doesn't already know:
God is big. God is round.
The force to be reckoned with—
The face of our latent prayers.
God is small as the mouse
standing in our shadows.
The word we'll never grock
the meaning of—The problem
we'll never solve. God is in
the refrigerator magnet holding
his smudged drawing up:
Sun and stars and people, colored-in
like an untenable fence of gravity.

   God is flawed and imperfect.
The static at the other end
of the dial tone of the insane.
A bad joke someone told
at the table. The handiwork of rain
that shakes out from an umbrella.
The absence at the grave of someone
we once knew. And in the "Oh"
of pain that we can't begin to name.
My son is sure there is a language
to explain everything—God is the relic

he sets in his pocket—The watermark
of breath he leaves at the window,
so we can see the perfectly
imperfect constellations.

Oceans of Love
Emelia Wade

HE   is a light house
Guiding ships to shore when Lost
Disappears then circles back
Never to be forgotten
Always to be remembered
Shipwrecked
Following SIN like an arrow to a compass
Spinning fast
Dizzy from the angry waves of the ocean
Sick from the crash, onto an unknown island

The notion of being misunderstood by natives
But HE has found me
Leading me towards the light
Finding comfort in the welcoming warmth of seeing HIM
alone on top of the hill

Waiting for me
A shipwrecked sailor
Not Lost but found
HE is a light house
Filled with Oceans of Love.

My Father's Frying Pan
KC Bosch

I never asked him: do you
respect me? Do I make you proud?

He could answer any question
like he was still wearing

his orange flight suit
with a slide rule in a leg pouch.

He was my map,
a chart he never had.

I'm still trying to find my way
as the onions sizzle

and I chop peppers.
Tears have smeared the ink.

I held him in my hands;
I carried him around.

He didn't weigh much
more than his frying pan.

Functional not fancy,
straightforward, indestructible:

seasoned and aged a
thousand meals black.

Mama
Nadia Boudidah

Today she's not waiting for me
Lost about how to begin
This task, this life, ahead without her.
What would you change yourself into?
I flounder
Without you
The roaring in my ears, I knew
Wasn't going to stop.
It was the crashing of the petrified forest
Stone dreams?
I knew, in a manner that went
Beyond the meaning of words
My heart remembers
Beyond the depths of the heart
The immutable passion
The uncomplicated affection
The unconditional security
That passed between us

Indestructible.

Grandmother Magic, 13 August 1977
Darlene Anita Scott

Lye is caustic.
Do not let it touch your skin.

Hem pants, can tomatoes,
grow peaches, mix the soap.

Heat gently.

Avoid inhaling fumes, ventilate and cover your eyes
with glass, goggles, something.

Mix vigorously.

Smell of something singed
its heat covers me in a sweat membrane, a
caul that dupes grains of sand to dance the stinging dance, twists
my skirt to a winding sheet, gossamer
tart seducing my meantime carelessly; live wine-
sipping well in this meantime.

Hem pants, can tomatoes,
Pick peaches, cut the soap.

I worry that I have dreamt this
better than I knew it: *The hardest step*
will be knowing when it's done.

Hem pants, can tomatoes,
can peaches, share the soap.

Matchstick bridges sturdy my soul
best they can
and in this giving become weighted
with the souls who follow, fail, fall

destroy the way
back.

The One Breath
W.F. Lantry

Prayer is nothing but the inhaling and exhaling
of the one breath of the universe.
—Hildegard of Bingen

Silence in candlelight. Red incense burns
in stillness, and the swirling smoke is caught
in columns made of warmed encompassed air.
She walks towards the center, pauses, waits,
and draws a single breath, inclined to prayer,
so motionless it seems her figure's wrought
from marble or from flowing bronze, but she,

the focus of this earth's vitality
for just this moment, lifts her voice and sings.
How can the formless air, remade to sound,
possess such beauty? Her voice recreates
the harmony we'd thought we'd lost, or found
only in dreams or visions darkness brings
and each dawn banishes. But even here

in this shared place, those visions reappear
or we recover something else. Our breath
flows in with hers: the universe seems one,
united in that beauty, as if gates,
once closed, had been reopened and the sun
flowed once again through gardens, where no death
is mournful, where an endless fire burns.

Acknowledgments

Cynthia Atkins lives in Virginia. "God's Watermark" first appeared in *Chelsea 80*. This poem can also be found in her book *Psyche's Weathers* (WordTech Communications, 2007) along with "Cold Feet." Her most recent book is *In the Event of Full Disclosure* (WordTech Communications, 2013).

William Auten lives in Ventura, California. His poems "Waste-deep in Sand" and "Battery" appear here for the first time.

Jacqueline Bishop was raised in Jamaica and now lives in New York. Her first book of poems is *Fauna* (Peepel Tree Press, 2006). Her most recent book of poetry is *Snapshots from Istanbul* (Peepel Tree Press, 2009). "Fire Builder" first appeared in *Moko Caribbean Arts and Letters*. Her poems "New World Finches" and "Wandering Jew" appear here for the first time.

KC Bosch lives and writes in Rappahannock County, Virginia. His poem "Eating Contest in a Third World Diner" first appeared at *vox poetica*. "The Harbor Inn" and "My Father's Frying Pan" were first published at *Dead Mule*.

Nadia Boudidah lives in Kairouan, Tunisia. Her poem "Mama" appears here for the first time.

Angela M. Carter hales from Virginia (with a lengthy sojourn in Bath, England, in the middle). Her poems "Revisiting Past Seasons," "Splinter," and "Woman at the Auction House" are part of her collection *Memory Chose a Woman's Body* (unbound CONTENT, 2014).

Dikson comes from Zimbabwe and performs his poetry internationally. A media version of "Limbo" is available on YouTube; this is its first print appearance.

J. Indigo Eriksen has come to Virginia after living in such places as Colorado, Oregon, California, Guatemala and Mexico. Her poems "Enter the House: Desert Ode," "Heartbeat," and "Walt Whitman: A Tribute" appear here for the first time.

Mark Fitzgerald teaches at the University of Maryland. "Big-Rig through Stolen Night" and "Millennium Retribution in Key West" come from his first book, *By Way of Dust and Rain* (Cinnamon Press, 2010). "Before and After" appears here for the first time.

Stan Galloway grew up in the Pacific Northwest but now calls Virginia home. "World's First Blues" was first published at *Scarlet Literary Magazine*. "Failed Romance" first appeared at *vox poetica*. "Carnival" comes from his first collection, *Just Married* (unbound CONTENT, 2013).

Kelly Grieco lives in Virginia. Her poems "For K," "Listening Ears," and "To Do:" are printed here for the first time.

John Hoppenthaler teaches creative writing at East Carolina University. His books, *Lives of Water* and *Anticipate the Coming Reservoir* (Carnegie Mellon University Press, 2003 and 2008) predate his forthcoming book, *Domestic Garden* (Carnegie Mellon University Press, 2015) and he edits "A Poetry Congeries" for Connotation Press: An Online Artifact. His poem "Buffeted" comes from *Anticipate the Coming Reservoir*. "Domestic Garden" first appeared in *The Laurel Review*, and "Fable with Pekin Ducks" appeared in *The Literary Review*.

Julie Ellinger Hunt resides in New Jersey. Her poem "Hudson County Girl" first appeared at *vox poetica* and "Somewhere in New Mexico" at *The Momo Reader*; both are printed in her second book, *In New Jersey* (unbound CONTENT, 2011). "Set Adrift" is printed here for the first time.

m. e. jackson lives retired in Virginia. Her poem "Collapse of Silver Bridge" first appeared in *Rappahannock Voices* (Riverside Writers, 2014). "Poetic Vision" and "Wolf at the Door" are printed here for the first time.

Sarah Kennedy teaches and writes at Mary Baldwin College in Virginia. Author of numerous books, award-winning *Flow Blue* (Elixer Press Prize in Poetry, 2002) and *Exposure* (Cleveland State University Press Winner, 2003) precede *The Gold Thread* (Elixer, 2013) from which her poems "The Changeling," "Julian, in Her Cell: 1405," and "One True Story" come.

Sana Khalesi lives in Shiraz, Iran. "Paris-Shiraz" first appeared at *The Camel Saloon*. "No Country for Young 'I'" and "Teary Queene" appear here for the first time.

Kate Lahey is a Newfoundland writer living in London, England. Her poems "The Cellar Door," "The Meaning of Melanin" and "A Room of One's Own" appear here for the first time.

Brandon Lamson writes from Houston, Texas. His poems "Metallica Burns on the Altar of the Viking Rockstar," "Rose M. Singer," and "Starship Tahiti," come from *Starship Tahiti: Poems* (University of Massachusetts Press, 2013, reprinted with permission of the publisher).

W.F. Lantry, a native of San Diego, writes from Washington, D.C. His poetry is published in *The Language of Birds*, a chapbook (Finishing Line, 2011) and *The Structure of Desire* (Little Red Tree, 2012) where "Rainbow Bridge" and "Pilgrimage" are printed. "Rainbow Bridge" first appeared in *Cha: An Asian Literary Journal* and "Pilgrimage" first appeared in *CutBank* where it won the 2010 Patricia Goedicke Prize in Poetry. "The One Breath" appears here for the first time.

John Lezcano lives in Jeffersonton, Virginia. His poems "Alabama Sunshine," "I've Heard of You," and "The (Poe)t" are printed here for the first time.

Annmarie Lockhart lives in Englewood, NJ, where she founded and continues to manage both *vox poetica* and its print sister, unbound CONTENT. Her poems "Guided by Stars and Glass," "Hopscotch Pedigree," and "Overheard at a Bar in New York City" appear here for the first time.

Don Maclennan lived from the age of 8 in South Africa. His book *Notes from a Rhenish Mission* (Carapace, 2001) was featured via DVD at the festival. Sections 3, 18, and 20 are reprinted here by permission. He published 21 books of poetry before his death in 2009.

Lynn Martin lives and performs her poetry in Virginia. "Carolina Handler" first appeared in *Poetry Northwest*; "After Sandy Hook" and "Continental Drift" appear here for the first time.

Sara Robinson lives near Charlottesville, Virginia. "Leaving Elkton" and "Sanjaray, Afghanistan" can be found in her book *Two Little Girls in a Wading Pool* (Cedar Creek, 2012). "Capote and Brando Talk Over Drinks" appeared in her latest poetry book, *Stones for Words* (Cedar Creek, 2014).

Darlene Anita Scott writes from Richmond, Virginia. "Wishing Tree, 6 June 1977" first appeared in a slightly different version in *the jonestown report*. "Disappearance, 26 July 1977" and "Grandmother Magic, 13 August 1977" appear here for the first time. All of these poems are part of a project exploring the psychology of Jonestown.

Julian Stannard teaches at the University of Winchester, after a significant teaching stay in Genoa, Italy. "Valleys Breathe, Heaven & Earth Move Together" and "Well-Regulated Dumplings Are Going Upwards" come from his book *The Parrots of Villa Gruber Discover Lapis Lazuli*. His poem "The Gargantuan Muffin Beauty Contest" first appeared in *Poetry* (Chicago).

Toni Stuart is a South African poetry writer, performer and developer. Her poems "The Cape Doctor," "For Imad," and "How" are published here for the first time.

Chad Trevitte lives in Virginia, though most Virginians can tell he grew up farther south (Tennessee) when he speaks. His poems "*Invasion of the Body Snatchers*" and "*Shane*" are from a sonnet series in progress based on classic movies. Along with his poem "Baudelaire," these poems see print here for the first time.

Emelia Wade has lived in a number of countries and now resides in Virginia. Her poems "Good Morning," "Oceans of Love," and "Stranger" are printed here for the first time.

Justin Walmsley currently lives in the Toronto area of Canada, after a two-year tour of England and Scotland. His poems "Swim" and "Mannlicher Rackenakt" appear here for the first time.

Lesley Wheeler writes from Lexington, Virginia. "Earth-Two Sonnet" first appeared at *Unsplendid* and can be found in *The Receptionist and Other Tales* (Aqueduct Press, 2012). "Scholarship Girl, 1953" appears in her chapbook *Scholarship Girl* (Finishing Line, 2007) and *Heterotopia*

(Barrow Street, 2010). "Dead Poet in the Passenger Seat" first appeared at *Prairie Schooner*.

Timothy Wisniewski comes from Fredericksburg, Virginia. His poem "My Rappaccini's Daughter" first appeared in the *Philomathean*. "Been Loving All My Life" and "The Last Night" appear here for the first time.

Phillippa Yaa de Villiers writes from Johannesburg, South Africa, where she is the 2014 Commonwealth Poet. "Tongue," the leading poem of this book, is printed here for the first time. Her poems "Stolen Rivers" and "Anthem" first appeared in *Beyond Words*.

Nicole Yurcaba lives in West Virginia where she teaches (Eastern West Virginia Community and Technical College), farms, and hunts. Her poems "Out Here in the Country" and "Night Vigil" appeared at *vox poetica*, and can be found in her book *Backwoods and Back Words* (unbound CONTENT, 2014). "Letter to My Grandfather" appears here for the first time, and is forthcoming in *Ukrainian Daze* (Unbound Content, 2015).

Selected Titles Published by Unbound Content

A Bank Robber's Bad Luck With His Ex-Girlfriend
By KJ Hannah Greenberg

A Strange Frenzy
By Dom Gabrielli

At Age Twenty
By Maxwell Baumbach

Assumption
Earthmover
By Jim Davis

Before the Great Troubling
Our Locust Years
By Corey Mesler

Elegy
By Raphaela Willington

Inspiration 2 Smile
By Nate Spears

In New Jersey
By Julie Ellinger Hunt

Painting Czeslawa Kwoka: Honoring Children of the Holocaust
By Theresa Senato Edwards and Lori Schreiner

Saltian
By Alice Shapiro

The Pomegranate Papers
This is how honey runs
Wednesday
By Cassie Premo Steele

www.ingramcontent.com/pod-product-compliance
Lightning Source LLC
Chambersburg PA
CBHW071716090426
42738CB00009B/1795